Juggling Family Life

A STEP-BY-STEP GUIDE TO STRESS-FREE PARENTING

Erin A. Kurt, B.Ed.

ISBN: 1-4392-3252-0
ISBN-13: 9781439232521

Visit www.booksurge.com to order additional copies.

Table of Contents

Introduction v

Part 1: Getting Discipline Right

Chapter One

 Discipline 3
 Three Types of Discipline 5
 The Permissive Method 11
 The Punitive Method 14
 The "Mishmash" Method 17
 The Democratic Method 18
 Making Things Real Clear 23

Chapter Two

 The Process of Changing Over 27
 Tricks of the Trade 33
 Let the Training Begin 40
 How to Proceed 50

Chapter Three

 Warding Off Common Problems 57
 Homework 58
 Allowances 62
 Grocery Shopping 65
 Dining Out/Restaurants 68
 Chores a.k.a. Teamwork Tasks 71
 Bedtime 78
 Television Privileges 82

Part 2: Family Time

Chapter Four

Making Time for Family 89

Dinner Time 92

Ideas for Family Interaction 96

One on One Time 98

Family Calendars 99

Alone Time is Important Too 100

Part 3: You

Chapter Five

All About You 105

Life Circle 107

Final Summary 113

Appendix - My Responses to the Scenarios 115

Introduction

Family life can definitely be a juggling act. We are living in a world that is faster paced than when we were children and sometimes we can feel like we are hamsters running on exercise wheels. In addition to this faster pace we have children who need our attention and guidance so that they are able to deal with the complex world they live in today. Many parents are finding it increasingly difficult to juggle everything that needs to get done. At the same time parents know they need more balance in their lives but believe there are just not enough hours in a day to get things done AND have downtime.

Well, if this is how you have been feeling, let me assure you that you have picked up the right book. In here you will find a guide on how to accomplish all that you need to and still have time left over to spend with yourself, your partner and your children. This book is different than all the rest of the parenting books out there. You will not have to spend hours reading only to be left with a feeling that everything you need to do in order to regain balance in your family's life is too overwhelming. After reading this book you will feel confident and empowered. Everything will seem possible because I teach you how to make it so. All that is mentioned is simple and efficient, yet totally effective.

Family dynamics have literally been of interest to me since I was a small child. I have always cared deeply about children, parents, and communities. My life's path has directed me in a way that not only prepared me to write this book, but has made my life one that is blissful. It is through my years of working with children and families, as well as raising my own child that I have gained the wisdom I feel is so important to share. My vast experience as a teacher has allowed me to witness all sorts of family dynamics, and the ramifications, both good and bad, of certain parenting styles. I have helped many, many parents deal successfully with specific and general parenting problems, and most importantly, have been able to work with thousands, and I do mean thousands of children who showed me each and every day what they really needed and desired.

Through my experiences I became increasingly aware of three main areas that either made families work or not work: Discipline, Family time, and You time. These are three areas that I personally keep in mind on a daily basis and are what make my family life truly rewarding and fulfilling. As a teacher I gained the hearts of children and parents alike because I was able to make the year with me a truly meaningful one. The cards and letters I received each year made me aware that what I was intending on doing was being accomplished on a very deep level. I am thrilled to say that by using the same techniques as I did in the classroom I have managed to have an absolutely incredible family life. My relationship with my son is unbelievably precious. Having special moments with my husband is easy and fun, and, in addition to this, I am able to spend quality time with myself and my girlfriends – something so very important. How do I do this? The answers are in this book.

Different than other parenting books, I focus less on theory and more on what works and what doesn't. I've sectioned the book into three parts because I feel there are three very important areas that need to be looked at when thinking of changing the dynamics of your family. The sections are positioned in a particular order for a simple reason: the first topic must be dealt with before the second and third can be achieved. Without discipline firmly established, the other two topics of "Family Traditions" and "You" will not easily be achievable, and in turn will have less impact on the all around dynamics of your family.

In the first section of the book I will explain four easy steps to discipline, and will have you so trained to use them that when you are ready to begin using the techniques with your children, the steps will come automatically to you. It is through all of my teaching experience that I was able to formulate a simple, yet truly effective way to discipline that leaves a child's self-esteem in tact, and helps them learn many lessons at the same time. Once I formulated this system of discipline I was lucky enough to use it successfully with my students, the children I nannied, and now, my own child. In the second part of the book I will offer you suggestions as to some traditions you and your family can begin together, and help you find your own special ones too, so that a greater bond is established between all members of your family. Finally, in the last section, I will help you realize that by paying attention to your own personal needs and wants you will be able to feel whole, even within all the demands that come from being a parent. I will show you how to easily regain balance in your life and at the same time, model what a healthy lifestyle is to your children. If you put into practise the ideas I suggest in this book, I have no doubt that you will have the family life you have always desired.

There are two ways you can use this book. One way is to read through the whole book and then go back and focus on each section at a time. The second alternative is to read the first section and begin putting into action all the tricks I give you. After reading this section you might need three months of implementing the techniques before you move on to the second part. This is absolutely fine. Give yourself the time to feel confident using the techniques, and enough time to see real results in your children. Only then should you try adding the suggestions from the other two parts.

Alright, are you ready? Be prepared to see a huge transformation in your family. Being a great parent and having a happy family life is easier than you might think!

PART I

Getting Discipline Right

Chapter One

DISCIPLINE

Whaaaaaaaaaaaa!, Mom, Brian hit me.

He hit me first.

I was watching my favourite show and he changed the channel.

Did not.

Did too.

(Punch, hit, Punch, hit)

Brrring! (phone rings)

Hello? Thirty cookies for Friday? Okay.

Mom!!!!!!!!!!!!!!!!!!!!!!!

Can you hold on a second? Stop it, before I come in there! Sorry, oh sure, I can be a volunteer for that.

Whaaaaaaaaaaaa! Mom, HELP! (Sons hitting and punching each other beside you)

Brenda, I'm sorry, I have to go. You go to your room and you sit down at the table for supper because you have to be at your soccer game in 15 minutes!

I'm not going to my room. I didn't do anything wrong.

You hit your brother.

I did not.

Yes, you did.
I did not! You never believe me.
Look, GO TO YOUR ROOM and DON'T ARGUE!
I'm not going; it's not fair. I want to eat.
Ahhhh! Just sit down quickly. CAN'T YOU TWO JUST GIVE ME A BREAK FOR ONCE?

Does this scenario seem familiar to you? Have you ever wondered what to do in a situation like this, but came up with no quick solution so you yelled instead? Have you ever felt exasperated and hopeless and wondered why nobody ever trained you to deal with situations like the above example, or prevent them from happening at all? Or, have you ever thought to yourself, "Why can't I have a break from chaos just once?" Well you can! It's easier than you think to end all the chaos; to discipline. You just need the right tools. But, the tools can't be complicated or confusing because you don't have much time. They have to be sensible, easy, and undeniably proven to work. You don't want to have to think back to that book you read and try to remember what the author suggested to do in this very type of situation; you want to be able to react right away, confidently, easily and effortlessly. Read on to find out how this can be achieved.

THREE TYPES OF DISCIPLINE

Before I can teach you the tools for effective discipline, I need to help you realize what current method of discipline it is that you are using. This is extremely important because you have to look carefully at what you are doing presently and the response you are getting, or not getting, and understand why it has not been effective. If you don't realize why your approach hasn't been working for you, you will probably end up using a mixed approach of mine and yours, and this won't work. If you are reading this before you have children, in order to prepare, simply think back to what methods your parents used. People tend to fall back on what they know and are used to in times of stress, therefore, even if you disagree with your parent's style of discipline, the tendency will be for you to use it with your own children unless you are trained to use a different style.

I will use an example to demonstrate how integration of my method and yours does not work. I had a boy in one of my classes named Adam who was never getting his homework done, acted out in class often, had a mess around his desk that looked like a paper explosion had gone off, and was very aggressive when faced with experiencing any type of consequence. I called the parents to set up a meeting. At the meeting we discussed Adam's behaviours and they nodded their heads in agreement. His father said, "That's Adam. He is exactly the same way at home. Our other two children are fine. They do well in school and are tidy and organized. We never have to ask them to do anything, they just do it. We don't know what to do." I asked them what methods of discipline they were using. The mother said, "We don't take any bad mouthing in our house. He knows that if he talks back after we have told him to do something he will get in huge trouble." I then asked what "huge trouble" meant and they said, "Well, he first gets a real good talking to and then we send him to his room and he stays there all night without TV or seeing his friends." I wanted to see the interaction between Adam and his parents so I invited Adam in from the hallway. As soon as Adam entered the room his father said firmly, "Hurry up, get over here and sit down."

I didn't even have time to start talking to Adam before his mother began lecturing and telling him that his behaviour was going to stop today. She said how embarrassed they were to have been called to the school to hear about the stupid things he was doing in class. They then took him over to his desk and literally dumped out the contents. As I watched this, the falling crumpled papers seemed to express what Adam must have been feeling on the inside at this point; crumpled up from embarrassment. I did not enjoy seeing this, but it gave me great insight into how things were working at home. I asked everyone to come back and sit down.

"Adam," I questioned, "do you understand why I asked your parents to come here for a meeting?"

He said, "Cuz I've been bad".

I rephrased that and said, "Because some of your behaviours have been unacceptable, yes." I continued by saying, "Adam, your behaviours need to stop because they are not helping you or the others in the class. It's disruptive to everyone's learning and I can't let this happen because I am responsible for creating a positive learning environment in the classroom. At the beginning of the year, I went over my expectations about behaviour and homework. Do you remember them?"

"I don't know," replied Adam.

"Well, what are you supposed to do when you want to say something?"

"Put up my hand."

"Yes, great. And, what are you supposed to do when I hand out a loose worksheet?"

"Put it in my binder."

"Can you be more specific about *when* you are supposed to put it in your binder?"

"Right away."

"Perfect! And as for homework, what are the consequences of not having your homework finished?"

"We stay after school."

"Right, you stay after school until it's done. Now, you are an extremely intelligent young man. Because of that, I have full confidence that you are capable of finishing your homework in an hour each night. That would leave you the rest of the night to do what you choose. What would you choose to do if you had the whole night free after finishing your homework?"

"I don't know, watch TV."

"Would you be able to play with David for a while?"

"Yeah, I guess."

"How about kicking around a soccer ball with your dad?"

"Yeah, right, that would be the day. They just like to lock me in my room at night."

(I note this in order to discuss it with his parents later)

"You need to make a choice right now. You can follow the classroom rules about putting your hand up, keeping your desk organized and completing homework or you will be asked to leave the room and work in another space for a day at a time. What is your choice?"

"Some choice. It's like you're forcing me to do what you want."

(He's trying to engage me in a discussion about how hard off he is. I don't engage.)

"This is not up for discussion. Did you understand what I asked you?"

"Yeah, but those aren't choices."

(Adam is really intelligent and he loves to debate like this. So I cut him off so he can cool down)

"You can make a choice now, or go outside and spend 10 minutes making your decision."

"I'll go outside."

"Alright, I'll call you back in 10 minutes."

I should mention that during the latter part of my discussion, Adam's parents were trying to intervene by yelling at him. I gave them a signal to back off for a bit so they did. However, as soon as he left, they said, "He shouldn't be allowed to make the decisions. He is just being belligerent." I explained that he was trying to engage me in a full blown discussion that would leave everyone feeling exhausted and frustrated. He was feeling a bit squeezed so I sent him off allowing him to make that choice. By having him make the choice, I helped him feel less squeezed. I explained that this didn't mean he was off the hook on making his choice about classroom rules.

With Adam waiting outside, I went over the homework schedule that I usually suggest parents follow at home. After discussing their nightly schedule, we agreed that Adam would go straight home from school and between 4:00 and 4:30 he would have a snack in the kitchen.

I asked his mom if there was a food he particularly liked and she said that he adored brownies. She agreed that for the next little while she would have a healthy version of brownies waiting for him along with an apple or another vegetable/ fruit snack. At 4:30 he would begin his homework in their office with a computer and would have an hour to be able to ask her for help if he needed any. After the hour, she would ask him to show her his agenda and then go through and display each completed assignment. She would offer some form of praise and also guidance if she thought something could be neater. Completion *and* neatness were to be stressed. At this time she would get him to pack up his books in his back pack, put it by the door, give him some form of physical praise such as a shoulder squeeze, hug, stroke of the head, and say, "What are you choosing to do before supper at 6:30?" Turning to Adam's father, I reminded him of how Adam had responded when I asked him about kicking the soccer ball around. I suggested that he invite Adam out to the garage to build something or take him to the baseball diamond to hit balls or even take him to watch a local game at the stadium. "Yeah, I can do that," he said.

Adam's parents also told me they have a rule about the kids filling the dishwasher after dinner, so I told them to state clearly to Adam that he was still expected to fill the dishwasher but after that, the night was free for him to do what he wanted. The parents seemed very confident that this was a good plan. I knew they would stick to it because of their ability to be firm. I asked them to try it for two weeks and to let me know how things went.

We had finished our conversation in ten minutes so I went outside to invite Adam back in and repeated my question matter of factly.

"So, what is your choice?"

Adam replied, "I'll follow the rules," with a bit of attitude, but I didn't make an issue out of it. I would wait and see if he really meant it tomorrow. Our talk was over, the parents were ready to discuss their plan with him after dinner that night and the slate was clean between him and me.

Everything seems fine now, doesn't it? The parents have new tools, Adam has agreed to follow the rules, and his parents will be giving him more positive attention. What could go wrong?

The next day Adam came in quietly and put his binders in his desk. We started the day by having a discussion about the differences between communism and democracy. Adam was always interested in political topics. He began to speak out of turn so I immediately looked at him and raised my hand. He quickly remembered what he had promised and raised his hand. That day was fantastic. He followed all the rules and his classroom behaviour was exceptional, yet I sensed he was a bit depressed. I found this odd. A few days after I realized this, Adam began coming to school without his homework finished. His behaviour continued to be pleasant but now he was almost withdrawn, and wasn't speaking much. I decided to call his parents. When I asked his mother how things were going she said, "Well, the first night was fine, and then the next night he came home from school without books he needed so I told him to get his ass back to school and get them."

"And did he do his work when he got home without being told?" I asked.

"Are you kidding? He sat on the couch like a lump and we had a huge argument about being responsible and not keeping his promises. Then his dad came home and sent him to his room for the night."

I was thinking, "Oh boy, Adam's behaviour in class makes sense now." I needed to have a conversation with Adam's parents about some of the errors they were making with our plan.

As you can see, I can give you all the tools in the world , but if you use them while repeating your old patterns, the tools will be ineffective and you will be left feeling even more frustrated and exasperated than before. Adam's parents were right in giving him consequences, however, the consequences were harsh and given with an angry tone. In addition to this, they needed to refrain from attacking him as a person but concentrate on describing his behaviours. Finally, they needed to be consistent. After the huge argument, they forgot all about keeping him on his homework schedule. His father however, tried asking him to kick a soccer ball around, but by this time, Adam was resentful and refused. The method they were using was definitely what I would call the "Mishmash" method: a mixture of all three approaches to discipline.

Okay, let's begin looking at the three methods of discipline that many psychologists have labelled. Different names have been attached to these methods, but I have chosen to refer to the three names I feel best represent each style. While reading the following real- life examples of each method, see if you can identify with any of the actions or words described in each situation. These are examples I have personally witnessed, and are not over dramatized, believe me! Try to see which method best illustrates your family dynamics. This may be a difficult task, but trust me, it's really necessary if you want to see a real difference in your children's behaviour and in turn your family life.

THE PERMISSIVE METHOD

This method involves a lot of talking and explaining. Unfortunately, it doesn't work because children are concrete learners and have egocentric thought, particularly from ages 2-7 years old. Although many parents have the right intention, this talking method does not work; children need direct, concrete experience of a consequence to understand that what they did or are doing is not acceptable.

Not knowing what age your children are, I will give you real examples of a permissive style of parenting within each developmental level. This way, you will be able to see more clearly if this is in fact how you tend to discipline.

Toddler

Mary knows it's about time for her son Riley to have a snack. She asks Riley what he wants to eat. He runs away giggling. She repeats her question a little louder this time so he can hear her from where he is. She hears no reply. Mary walks around the house calling his name and finally finds him laughing behind a door. She repeats the question again and begins an explanation as to why having a snack now is important.

He says, "I want Jell-O."

Mary tells him that Jell-O is not a snack.

"I want Jell-O!" he screams.

"You can't have Jell-O. You can have a peanut butter sandwich," she says sweetly trying to entice him.

"No, I want Jell-O!" he screams louder.

"Sweetie, you need to be healthy and mommy wants you to eat, so decide now or I'll send you to your room with no snack at all."

Riley starts crying while stuttering, "I – want - Jell-O"

She hates seeing him cry and really wants him to eat something. She thinks, "I guess Jell-O is better than nothing. I just won't give him dessert tonight." She hugs him tight and says, "Alright Sweetie, calm down. You don't need to cry. We'll get you some Jell-O, but that means no dessert tonight, okay?"

Sniff, Sniff, "Okay."

Elementary School-aged Child

The time is 3:30pm and Linda is picking up her child from school. Her daughter, Sarah, asks if she can play on the outdoor equipment with her friends for a while. She says, "Sure, but only for half an hour."

Linda sits with other parents on the bench while watching the children play. She notices that the children are playing tag.

She feels worried that the game is not safe to do on this type of equipment.

"Sarah," she calls, "I don't think you should be playing tag on that equipment."

Sarah ignores her and continues playing.

"Sarah, I think you should play that on the ground."

"We're okay, mom, don't worry," Sarah replies.

Linda continues watching and talking with the other parents, but still feels uneasy.

"Sarah…"

"What?" Sarah asks, now irritated.

"I really wish you'd play that on the ground. Come on, it's not worth getting a broken arm. Come on, play down here."

All of a sudden she hears someone crying and realizes a little boy was tagged too hard and fell off the equipment. She runs to help and then tells Sarah it's time to go home. On the way home she says to her, "See? I told you it wasn't safe. You never listen. You need to listen to me when I tell you something isn't safe."

Teenager

Mandie, a teenager, has been watching TV for two hours and her mother knows she has a big assignment due in Language Arts the next day.

She calls, "Mandie, don't you have an assignment due tomorrow? Turn off the TV now, please."

She still hears the TV after 5 minutes so she calls again. "Mandie! Turn off the TV, and work on your assignment."

After another 5 minutes she *still* hears the TV so she goes into the living room. "Mandie, I asked you to turn off the TV. You have a major assignment due tomorrow and you are going to be up all night again trying to finish it. If you turn the TV off I'll help you get started; I know that's the hardest part."

"Alright, already. I'll go to my room and work on it."

"Great, if you need any help, just ask, okay?"

Mandie doesn't respond. She walks slowly and reluctantly to her room and closes the door. She takes out her books then finds her library book inside one of them. She decides to read just a little bit before starting her assignment.

At 11:00pm Mandie's mother goes into her room to see how she's doing and finds her asleep with her book on her chest and the first page of her story lying on the floor. She wakes Mandie up.

"Mandie! Wake up!"

"What? I'm tired."

"You have to hand a story in tomorrow. What are you going to do?"

"I'll hand it in late."

"No, get up, you tell the story to me and I'll type it."

The mother stays up until 3:00am typing the story with Mandie.

The next morning Mandie is so tired she can't get up for school. Her mother lets her sleep until 10:00am then takes her to school.

Did any of these stories sound familiar to you? Did you recognize yourself or your children in any of these situations? Remember, these are just examples and there are definitely varying degrees of permissive parenting. However, in general, if you use a permissive style of parenting you lecture, give sermons, repeat, remind, use words like "I wish you would…", "I think you should…", "It would be nice if…", and give threats, but never follow through on them. You wonder why your children do things that you have asked them not to do many times.

THE PUNITIVE METHOD

Again, as with the Permissive Method, the Punitive Method has varying degrees. The following examples will illustrate the typical signs of a parent using the Punitive Method.

Toddler
Ben and his family are sitting at the dinner table. His mother was serving the food and he begins complaining right away.
   "I don't want that."
   "Ben, don't start. You will eat this."
   "I don't like it."
   "No complaining. Eat!"
   Ben sits with his arms folded and replies, "NO!"
   SLAP! Ben's father slaps him across the face and says, "Now, eat."
   Ben hangs his head and literally looks like he is crawling inside himself. His mother scoops some food on a fork for him and moves it towards his face.
   "Here," she says.
   Ben ends up eating most of what is on his plate.

Elementary School-aged Child
A mother is part of a boat racing team. Today is the big competition. She has had problems with her son before so she tells him to stay home. She'll be back at 7:00pm. The day is going well and she is having a great time with her team-mates. While standing around chatting between races, she sees her son ride up on his bicycle. She becomes furious and yells at him.
   "What the h—l are you doing here? I told you to stay home!"
   "I just came to say hi."
   "I don't care why you came. I told you to stay home!" she yells.
   Her son becomes embarrassed at being yelled at in front of her friends so he yells back.
   "You're a b—h!"
   Now, the mother is furious *and* embarrassed. She drags him away and proceeds to tell him that he is disrespectful and that she will not tolerate him talking to her like that in public. She says, "You are so

disrespectful. You can't talk to me like that. What a jerk you are for coming to my big day and spoiling it. You go home right now. You are NOT welcome here!"

Teenager
Jamie, 14 years old, just got invited to a co-ed party on Friday. She asks her parents if they can drive her.

"I am invited to a party on Friday. It starts at 8:00pm. Can you drive me?"

"Party? What party? You never asked permission to go to any party," says her mom.

"Sorry. Can I go?"

"Your mother and I will discuss it," replies her father.

Jaime's parents go into the kitchen and talk about whether she should go or not. They decide that she can go, but that they will pick her up at 10:00pm. They walk to Jaime's room and tell her their decision.

"We have decided that you can go but we're picking you up at 10:00pm."

"What? That's not fair!"

"Hey, we can tell you that you can't go. That is our final word. Do you want to go or not? We have to know now so we can plan our schedule," said her father.

"I can't believe you guys. You will let me baby-sit for you until 3:00am but I am only allowed to go to my very first party until 10:00pm."

"Keep arguing and we will just say no, Jaime."

"You guys are so unfair. You treat me like I'm a baby. I'm growing up you know, and you're gonna have to face that some day."

"Okay, I told you to quit arguing and you didn't. Now, you have lost your privilege to go. Think about how you talk to us next time you want something."

"I hate you!" screams Jaime.

Her parents leave and slam the door behind them.

These examples show a totally different method of parenting than the last one. Did you read these ones and connect with any part of them? Maybe you do or say similar things that these parents did?

In general, if you use this method of punitive discipline you tend to be inflexible, name call or use put down words, expect your children to behave perfectly if not close to perfect, or you give them little freedom, meaning not a lot of choice in decisions that directly affect them. You teach your rules by giving punishments.

THE "MISHMASH" METHOD

This method is one that I came up with after counselling many parents. We would agree on a plan and then they would come back and say it didn't work. After some discussion, I would recognize that they were trying to implement my ideas, but in a way they were most comfortable with. So, the "Mishmash Method" is when you mix the Permissive Method and the Punitive Method or the Democratic Method with either one. This is probably the most common method used in families today. Usually you start out using the Permissive Method of asking nicely, then repeating your request, then reminding again, then you give a lecture about why they should listen, and maybe you even try bribing them. Finally, you get so frustrated that you make a threat and eventually resort to yelling, slapping or spanking them.

Does this sound like your family dynamics? Maybe you are the parent who acts permissively and your partner finishes up things by acting punitively, or visa versa. You know the saying, "Wait until your father gets home."

In any case, this method does not work either. The most important thing about discipline is consistency. If you are using different discipline techniques than your partner, the children will end up being extremely confused and will play you against your partner in order to satisfy their wants and desires.

Let's look now at the method that is effective, less emotionally draining, takes less time and teaches your children responsibility, cooperation, independence, respect and self-control.

THE DEMOCRATIC METHOD

Although some talking is required in this method, it is action and tone that become the most important ingredients. A simple statement about what behaviour is required is spoken. Then, if the behaviour continues, a warning in the form of a question is given, and if the behaviour persists, a consequence is what follows. Along side this, encouragement, and positive touch is used to connect the parent and child.

This method works because it's simple, straight forward and creates a respectful relationship between you and your child. It also teaches your child how to solve problems as well as help them learn the very important lesson of responsibility. Think for a minute about your community. What characteristics would you want the people of your community to possess? Would you want them to be responsible? I'm sure you would want them to have jobs. Would you want them to be respectful? They would have to follow the laws and be polite, right? Finally, would you want them to know how to solve problems? You wouldn't want to have a lot of domestic abuse in your community would you? Would you want to see people fighting on the streets and hearing your next door neighbours argue every night? No, of course not.

Funny enough, no one wants these problems in their communities however, unless people are taught parenting skills, how do we expect to have safer, more caring communities? We cannot leave it solely up to the schools. These lessons need to be taught at home and reinforced at school. My life's mission is to teach as many people as I can the techniques to discipline in a democratic way so that the negative trends we see in our towns and cities of today begin to change and hopefully, eventually disappear. It's a big goal, but I fully believe that when families become stronger, communities become stronger.

How does this method work? Read the following examples and notice how the parents set limits, show confidence in their child, and if need be, give logical consequences and follow through on them.

Toddler
Anna has just begun walking and is touching everything in sight. She loves the look of all the buttons and knobs on the stereo. She pushes

the "ON" button, then plays with the radio channels and finally turns the volume up to maximum but doesn't know how to turn it down. Her father comes running and turns off the stereo, says a firm, "No" and moves her away. He then walks back to the kitchen where he is fixing the sink.

Anna sits on the ground thinking, "Wow, that sound scared me. I wonder what that big red button is for?" She remembers that her father told her no, but she really wants to touch that red button. She walks up to the stereo and pushes it. Nothing happens so she presses the power button. The volume is still at its maximum from before. Just as she is about to place her finger on the red button again, her father comes in, turns the stereo off and says in a matter-of–fact voice, "You can play in here without touching things or you can play in your room. What is your choice?" Anna responds, "Won't touch daddy." "Thank you, Anna," he replies and walks back to the kitchen.

Anna decides to play with her other toys for a while then begins looking around the room. Her eyes spot a new machine that she had never seen before. It was the DVD player her parents had bought last weekend. "Hmmm"…she thought, "I wonder what it's for?" She walks over to it, starts touching it but makes sure not to press any buttons. Anna's father happens to walk by when her hands are investigating the DVD player. He walks in the room, picks her up, carries her to her room and says, This is where you will play. We'll try the family room again later today. Anna really knew her father meant what he said. She was sad because she liked being around her family.

Anna's father has shown that he does what he says he will do and this means that he has earned Anna's respect. With respect, comes a willingness to comply, therefore next time her father warns her, she will comply right away instead of needing a consequence to help her understand.

Elementary School-aged Child

Juliana's birthday was yesterday. She had a big party and received many gifts. Her favourite present was a stuffed animal that had a string and handle attached to its head. She loved holding this and bouncing the animal because it's legs and arms would go flying up and down.

Juliana's parents called her for dinner. She came happily to the table with her toy bouncing beside her. As soon as her mother saw Juliana with the toy at the dinner table she said, "Juliana, you need to put your stuffed animal in your room or the family room. We don't bring toys to the table." "I'll just put it here beside me. I won't touch it." Her mother replied, "You were given two choices, did you hear them?" "Yes, but…" Before Juliana could engage in a discussion, her mother took the toy, put it away and said, "You can have your toy back tomorrow." Juliana tried to fuss and cry but her mother gave no attention to this. She was waiting to see if the crying would stop so she carried on with the serving of the meal. Juliana really wanted her toy so she continued crying and fussing. Her mother then said matter-of -factly, "You need to go to the living room to cool down. You can come back to the table in 5 minutes." Juliana was in quite a mood so she said a firm, "NO!" Her mother picked her up, took her to the living room and repeated, "You can come back and join us in five minutes." Juliana continued crying for a bit but eventually started hearing her family laughing. She waited for her mother to call her and then walked back to the table. Her mother touched her head lovingly and they ate dinner in peace. Soon, Juliana was sharing a funny experience that happened that day at school.

Once again, this parent has shown that what she says is what she does. This earns her respect and makes Juliana know that she should listen the first time her mother asks her to do something. Relations stay positive, lessons are learned, and encouragement is given in a positive way.

Teenager
Michelle, a very sociable 16 year old girl, loves hanging out with her friends after school. Her mother believes that because Michelle is an only child, this is very important. However, Michelle's grades have begun to slip. Her mother decides to have a chat with her.

She asks Michelle to sit down with her in the living room.

"Michelle, I know how important your friends are to you, however, I have noticed that your grades have been slipping. I know you are capable of figuring out a way to finish your homework *and* see your friends. Do you have any ideas as to how you could make this work?"

"I don't know. I feel like if I do all my homework then I will never have time to be with my friends. The teachers give too much…"

Before Michelle could get into her complaining mode, her mother said, "I spoke to your teachers and they told me that the homework they give shouldn't take more than 1 1/2 hours. So, an option would be to come home right after school, have a snack and some downtime for half an hour then begin your homework and work until you finish it. After that would be dinner and then you could spend time with your friends.

"I hate doing homework after school, I'm so tired."

"I know, that's how I feel right before I go work out at the gym. I have to push myself everyday but I feel great afterwards. Plus, I always try and remember that I will have the rest of my night free to read or watch my favourite TV shows. We are going to try this for two weeks. Now, the one stipulation is that you are home by 8:30pm each night and I need to see an improvement in your grades. We'll talk again in two weeks about how things are going."

"8:30? Isn't that kind of early?"

"We'll see how these two weeks go. If you show you can increase your grades then we'll discuss 9:00pm, if you show you can't handle this we'll have to stick with 8:30pm.

The Democratic method works wonders for teenagers because they especially need to feel like they are respected, have an input and are loved. Here, Michelle can see her mom takes an interest in her life and cares about her. She senses that her mom is flexible yet respects the fact that she has set limits. This is strangely comforting to her and encourages her to do better.

Could you sense while reading these examples that both the children and parents were less agitated, upset, or angry than in the Punitive and Permissive situations? Did you notice that the parents never engaged in a debate, never repeated themselves ten times, never gave lectures, and didn't need to use put downs or spankings to teach their lesson? The lessons that these children learned were responsibility, cooperation, time management, and accountability. They all still feel loved by their parents and they feel a sense of security knowing what their parents' expectations are.

If you think back to the Permissive approach, the child is experiencing too much freedom and never any consequences. What are they learning? They learn that their parents serve them, their parents are responsible for solving their problems, and that rules are for other people, not them. Basically, they become quite self- centered. Children of permissive parents don't tend to learn responsibility and will always want to test their parents because they are trying to find out where the limits are and have fun while they're at it!

Think back now to the Punitive Approach. Children who experience punitive discipline learn that parents are responsible for solving their problems and that slapping or name-calling are the ways to solve problems. Often, these children will exhibit anger and stubbornness and will tend to react in a revengeful or rebellious way because they don't understand their parent's limits; they find them unfair or always changing based on how their parents feel that day or moment.

MAKING THINGS REAL CLEAR

We have all done and said things we wish we wouldn't have. Now is the time to acknowledge those things, realize that, as Maya Angelou once said, "You were doing the best that you knew how, and now that you know better, you'll do better." Knowledge means everything when it comes to discipline. I am positive that after reading even this much of the book, you feel more confident about disciplining your child.

Below are typical words or actions which represent particular methods of discipline. I want you to put a check beside each statement that resonates with you. For example, it might be a belief you have about discipline, a technique you have used before, words you have said to your child, or reactions you have received from your child. After doing this exercise, read the instructions to clearly establish which method of parenting you have been using. If you have a spouse, have him/her do this exercise also. It is important for both of you to discover your current method. Both of you need to realize what hasn't been working so you can avoid repeating the same ineffective patterns. Remember, we want the two of you to be on the same track; consistency is of the utmost importance.

1. You have to repeat your request several, if not more times _____

2. You use the words "wish" or "shouldn't" "I shouldn't have to repeat myself a hundred times" _____

3. Your children tend to ignore or tune you out when you request something _____

4. You explain, lecture, or give a speech to teach your rules _____

5. You often ignore bad behaviour in order not to cause a fight _____

6. You believe that consequences that upset your child cannot be effective_____

7. You sometimes bribe your child so their behaviour stops _____

8. You often give a threat but don't follow through _____

9. You have high, almost perfectionist expectations for your children's behaviour _____

10. You tend to give your children little freedom _____

11. You use words like, "Stop being such a jerk", "I don't like your attitude" _____

12. You believe that it's your job to control your children _____

13. You believe that children won't respect your rules unless they fear you a little _____

14. You believe that children will cooperate when they understand that cooperation is the right thing to do _____

15. Your children often challenge your rules _____

Now I want you to analyze your answers.

If you checked off most of the statements between numbers 1-8 you have been using the **Permissive Method** of discipline.

If you checked off most between numbers 9-15 you have been using the **Punitive Method** of discipline.

If you checked off some from statements 1-8 and some from statements 9-15 you have been using the **Mishmash Method**.

Summary

How does knowing the difference between parenting styles help you? The first step to having great discipline is recognizing what you are doing presently and understanding why it's not working for you. Once you know better you can quickly catch yourself when tempted to revert back to old patterns. For example, let's say you give a limited boundary to your child. Your child thinks it's unfair so he tries to begin an argument.

If you were using the Permissive style, you might be tempted to engage in that argument by trying to support your decision with a number of reasons why it's a good decision. You then remember that this will not work. You know you would be spending a long time arguing and would be left feeling exhausted and frustrated. Therefore, you choose to use the Democratic method.

If you were using the Punitive method, you might be tempted to say, "Quit the attitude, or I'll just cancel the whole thing." You remember though, that this won't get you anywhere. Your child would try to continue the argument and then you would probably say, "Okay, that's it, forget the whole thing, go to your room, I'm finished talking." Your child would leave feeling resentful and revengeful and this is not what you are going for. Therefore, you stop the words from rolling off your tongue and you choose the Democratic method.

Having now realized your parenting patterns, get ready to change them to ones that will work and will make life for you and your family more enjoyable!

Chapter Two

THE PROCESS OF CHANGING OVER

Now that you have discovered which style you have been using and why it hasn't been working, it's time to start training yourself to use the Democratic Method.

When using the Democratic Method, you must feel extremely confident about setting firm limits. What are limits? They are boundaries that show where you cannot go beyond without facing a consequence. Think for a moment about our democratic society. We have the right to drive a car however there are rules that are our boundaries. If we go beyond those boundaries by speeding, we face receiving a ticket or if severe enough like hitting someone while driving drunk, we can go to jail. These would be the consequences of not staying within the boundaries.

Societies need to have these limits or else they would be in chaos. Do we as adults test these limits? Yes, it's part of our human nature; we always like to see how far we can go. For example, have you ever run a yellow light? I'm sure you have, most people have. Why do we do this? Probably because we know not much will happen. We haven't experienced many reprimands for doing so therefore we continue doing it, with caution, of course. Only recently have people begun to watch themselves more as the lights turn yellow. Why? Because many cities have positioned cameras that take a photo of your license plate if you go through one too late. This leads to a consequence of receiving an expensive ticket and nobody wants that, so we are stopping more at yellow lights now.

Children test limits too, except they are doing it on a more consistent basis. They don't have the knowledge that adults possess therefore they are trying to figure out how their world works. They use their parents as their main resource. Lucky us!

It is inevitable that our children will test us. No matter how nice we are, or how strict we are, they will test us. Please understand that this is completely natural and they aren't doing it to hurt you. Think of it as your opportunity to teach them about life. It's a big job, isn't it? You are literally training your child to become a strong, self-assured person who is compassionate and respectful. This seems daunting, I know, but you wouldn't believe how simple it really is; you just need to learn some basic techniques.

Let's begin with an example from my life that demonstrates how I used this philosophy of providing limits and if needed, following through with consequences.

EXAMPLE OF USING LIMITS AND CONSEQUENCES

Years ago, I lived with a family of five in France. There were three boys in the family. I definitely took the role of their second mother because their real mother worked a lot. As soon as I began caring for the boys, they began to test me. I knew the schedule they were used to so I basically followed it, adjusting things here and there. The youngest of the three boys became quite defiant because he hadn't been told "No" much or hadn't had to experience many consequences.

The morning routine was getting to be a struggle so I sat him down one night and explained how every morning was going to work from now on. I told him in a matter-of-fact tone that tomorrow morning I would wake him up at 7:00am, he would come to the table to have breakfast until 7:30am, then he was expected to get dressed and brush his teeth. After that, he would have 15 minutes to watch his favourite cartoons. We would leave for school at 8:00am. Here's how the rest of the conversation went after my instructions.

Did you understand what I just said?

I don't have to do what you say."

You know what? I think you are a big boy now. I think you can get dressed by yourself and watch TV with your older brothers. Do you feel like you're a big boy now?

Yeah.

Yeah, I do too. So, let's review tomorrow's schedule. I'll wake you up at 7:00am. Then what do you do?

Get dressed?

Something comes first.

I eat breakfast.

Then you…

Get dressed and go watch TV.

There's one step before that.

I don't know.

You brush your teeth. We'll all leave for school at 8:00am.

After this, I played a quick game where I acted out what he would do and he had to tell me the time at which it would happen. Then we switched roles because he was having so much fun. I called out the times and he acted out what he would do. Lots of laughs were had.

I gave him a big hug after the game and said, "*See you tomorrow morning!*" in an excited voice.

The next morning I woke him up at 7:00am and he shuffled his feet to the table. He ate his breakfast nicely. At 7:30am I told him to look at the clock. Then I said, "*It's 7:30, what are you going to do now?*

Uh, get dressed.

And?

His brothers chimed in, "Brush your teeth"

He smiled because he liked how his brothers were in on it too. He hopped off his chair to walk to the bathroom with his brothers. They all had fun laughing and playing around in the bathroom. At 7:45am I called out the time and they rushed to the living room to watch cartoons. At 8:00am, I said, "*Time to go.*"

All the boys gathered their books and we walked to school together. When I dropped the youngest boy off at his classroom, he gave me a big kiss on the cheek and I smiled at him and said, "*Have a great day, big boy*".

I want to take a detailed look at this example. What techniques was I using from the Democratic Method?

1) I spoke with a matter-of-fact tone
2) I chose not to let him engage me in a debate
3) Instead, I expressed confidence in him
4) I gave specific times when he had to do something
5) I used physical touch to bond us

It is fantastic when this is all it takes. Sometimes, all you have to do is this and it will work. However, often the child will be good for a period of time and will then retest. This is exactly what occurred with this little boy.

Every morning went smoothly for the first week. Then came the weekend; of course the same schedule does not exist on the weekends so the youngest could get up and laze around like everyone else. Sunday night came and I decided to subtly remind him of our deal.

"*Have a great sleep, Sweetie. I'll see you at 7:00am.*"

The morning came and as promised, I was in his room at 7:00am. He was very tired and grumpy, but he got up. All the boys ate their breakfast. When it was 7:30am I said, "*7:30 boys!*" The two older ones got up and went to the bathroom. The younger one stayed at the table and said, "*You dress me today.*" I replied, "*That's your job. Now go on quickly so you can watch cartoons for a while.*" He was in a stubborn mood.

He retorted, "*You have to dress me or I'm going to tell my mom.*"

I changed to my matter of fact voice and said, "*Philippe, you have two choices. You can be a big boy and get dressed yourself and watch cartoons, or you can get dressed and not watch cartoons. What is your choice?*"

"*You dress me.*"

"*That's not an option. You need to go to your room for 4 minutes to think about whether you choose to get dressed and watch cartoons or get dressed and not be able to watch cartoons. I'll come back in 4 minutes.*"

He screamed, "*You dress me!*"

I then picked him up physically and carried him to his bedroom and closed the door. He banged and banged and called me every name in the book. After 4 minutes I opened the door and asked him if he was ready to make a choice. He started hitting me so I told him he would have to stay another four minutes in there or until he calmed down. He could knock on the door to show me he was ready. He continued screaming. I opened the door after 4 minutes and asked him in my matter of fact voice if he was ready. He didn't say yes, but he walked past me to the bathroom grumbling the whole way. He then proceeded to the bathroom, put on his clothes, walked to the TV and sat down with his brothers who were laughing hysterically at the cartoons. Soon, he started smiling and all was normal again.

At 8:00am I called, "*Time to go, boys!*" They all grabbed their bags and off we went.

Now, you're probably thinking to yourself. "*I thought she said this method was easier and quicker. It sure seemed like she put in a lot of effort to me!*"

There are a few points to mention here. First, I really didn't do a lot of talking, did I? And the things I did say didn't make me seem like I was out of control. Secondly, this experience taught Philippe many important lessons that not only helped with the morning routine, but would help in future situations. He knew now where my limits were and that

I didn't back down. He also realized that I don't argue either. After the commotion of that morning, he was left feeling capable and independent. He also learned how to take responsibility for his actions. Finally, he learned that it didn't make sense to continue screaming because he lost out on cartoon time with his older brothers.

There will be challenging times, believe me. Remember, it's natural for children to test. However, the number of times they will test will decrease and the intensity of their testing will greatly diminish.

In the next section, I am going to share some techniques with you. These techniques will help you feel confident the next time you have to discipline your child. They will also help ensure that your discipline is effective.

TRICKS OF THE TRADE

The title of this section is called, "Tricks of the Trade" because these are the techniques I learned while dealing with some really challenging kids throughout my teaching career. During my university teaching practicum I was given a very difficult class. The teachers who had taught this group of students before questioned the principal if this was such a good idea. They couldn't believe that the principal was giving a young university student such a difficult class. I had learned a lot of techniques in university and was anxious to try them out so I told everyone that I was fine with the position. After successfully teaching this class I felt like a pro! Even my university facilitator commented on how my discipline techniques were like that of an experienced teacher. Needless to say, I was full of confidence. The next September I got my first job. I would be teaching grades four, five and six. I was told to be aware that some of the students were quite difficult and that they had had three different teachers before me. I became instantly nervous. "Wow," I thought, "if experienced teachers couldn't handle them, how was I going to?" That year was unbelievably challenging. These students were masters at testing. They had gotten away with so much in the previous years and were not about to stop just yet.

I had students who were doing cartwheels in the classroom and students who would walk up to me and stand in my space in order to intimidate me. I had kids with learning disabilities, Tourrette's Syndrome, Schizophrenia, ADD, ADHD, and basically students who didn't want to follow rules. It didn't take long to gain the respect of the grade four's and five's, but the grade sixes were a different story. I tried talking to them, reasoning, offering rewards, yelling, giving punishments, and phoning their parents, however nothing worked. I had run out of ideas! I didn't know what to do next. I couldn't figure out why they acted respectful towards their homeroom teachers and not me.

One day, however, I received my answer. The students were being their usual selves. I was teaching and many were talking and fooling around. I lost my control and yelled, "I cannot believe you! I have been so generous with you. I have worked my butt off trying to make this topic exciting and you don't even appreciate it. Would you like it if

I handed you worksheets and just had you answer questions all period? I don't think so. Well, tomorrow, things are going to change. If anyone talks when I am teaching they will stay after school and finish a package that I will put together. If you waste my time, I will waste yours.

A girl who was near me, piped up and said something I will never forget. "Just do it!"

"Pardon?" I questioned while standing in a state of shock.

"Just do it finally. You always say these things, but just do it!"

My first feeling was one of embarrassment, but then it hit me. That was it. I was actually not following through on the consequences I had threatened in the past, or at least not consistently. I was being consistent with the grade fours and fives but for some reason I was hesitant to do this with the grade sixes. Perhaps I was nervous they would get worse if I enforced a consequence. Then they would *really* hate me. I felt like a bolt of lightning had hit me. I finally "got it".

This story has a happy ending. After that momentous day, I stuck to my word just like I had been doing with the other grades. Yes, they tested me, but only occasionally and if they did they experienced the consequence. At the same time, I loosened up a bit and began to bond with them by cracking a few jokes, and using positive, supportive touch. The last few months we were together were great. The principal even came in to observe the class and congratulated me on being able to manage this difficult class.

On the last day of school, we had a celebration for the grade sixes. They all stood in a line and we teachers shook each student's hand. To my surprise, the students were crying at having to leave me. We hugged and cried, both girls and boys. It was such an emotional moment. I will always be grateful to them, especially the wise girl who spoke up that day.

Economically my school district was going through difficult times that year and as a result I was declared surplus. Therefore I moved on to a new school. Strangely enough, every year after that, I worked for a different school. The reasons varied. I wanted to go teach in France, I wanted to teach in a different city, in the private system, or in an International school, which is how I ended up in Brazil. Some people thought I was crazy. "Don't you want to put down roots?" they'd ask.

My answer was simple. I wanted to experience teaching as many different children as I could.

I have taught children from extremely poor families, orphans living in an orphanage, children who came from dysfunctional families and those who came from families where the parents were exceptional. I have also had the opportunity to teach children who came from extremely wealthy families. These children had their own maid, driver, cell phone, you name it! You know what? Every single child from these varied circumstances needed the exact same type of discipline. Some to a lesser or greater degree, but in general, all tested, all needed limits, and all needed to experience consequences in order for them to learn respect and responsibility, and in turn, self-love.

I realized also, that the wealthy parents who were experiencing difficulties with their children had similar problems to the ones who weren't as wealthy. Of course, each case is specific because each family has their own dynamics. What I'm talking about is the fact that parents who were struggling with discipline, needed to learn the same techniques.

I always felt honoured when parents felt comfortable enough to ask me for advice. They would say things like, "I don't understand how you get him to do that for you. What am I not doing right?" or "I can't get her to do her homework. I have tried everything. What do I do?", "We're so frustrated with him, he just doesn't listen." or "You can't even imagine what our mornings and evenings are like. I am at a loss." I could definitely sympathize with them. I knew first hand that feeling of exasperation.

I have always loved interacting with parents but last year it became clear that I had to share the techniques I have learned with the people who have not been exposed to them. I was sitting with more and more parents who were so concerned about their children. It was like another bolt of lightning hit me one day and told me that this was to be my mission; to teach pregnant parents, new parents, parents of teens, new teachers, anyone who wanted to hear about some techniques that were tried, tested and absolutely worked.

Okay, enough chatting, let's get down to business. Here are "The Tricks of the Trade".

Trick #1 – Describe the behaviour you want

Example: You are talking with someone and your child is tugging at your shirt repeating, "Mom, mom, mom." You simply say, "Brandon, you need to wait until I'm done talking". This statement is better than, "Would you stop tugging at me already?" or "You are being a pain, stop it!"

We need to consistently *expect* good behaviour and respect. At the same time, we need to consistently *model* good behaviour and respect. We never want to belittle a child or shake their self-esteem. When you simply state the behaviour you want, the results are effective while leaving the child's esteem in tact.

Trick #2 – Use a normal, matter-of-fact voice

When you are giving a clear message about the behaviour you want, you need to keep the tone of your voice normal but state the message in a matter-of-fact way. If you use a frustrated tone or an angry tone, you are showing the child that they have shaken you. This will only intrigue them and in most situations will continue the behaviour because they see they can engage you in a debate or yelling match. In their minds, some attention is better than none.

Let's use the same example of Brandon tugging at your shirt. This time you say in a frustrated voice, "Wait until I'm done!" You can see how it just has a different feel to it; you show a lack of control. You can almost bet that Brandon's reaction will be to continue his behaviour or begin to whine so that he can engage you further.

Trick #3 – Give limited choices

Every human likes and needs to feel as if they are in control of their lives. We adults wouldn't like it if we were told what car we had to drive, what we had to eat, or what bank we had to deal with, would we? It is the same for children. The only difference is that you are an adult and have earned the right to make your own choices. You also have experience to help you make your choices. Too many choices leave a child feeling overwhelmed and insecure. The best thing here is to allow children to make choices, but within a limited framework.

Example: You are cooking breakfast and you feel like making eggs. You don't say, "What would you like for breakfast?" because they could say something you are not prepared to make. You wouldn't say, "What kind of eggs do you want?" because that too, would be overly time consuming if all your children wanted a different style. You would give a choice between two styles of eggs that you *were* prepared to make and offer them as your limited choices. For example, "I'm making eggs and toast this morning, would you like scrambled or hard-boiled?" This way, the child will feel like she has some control over her breakfast.

Giving limited choices should also be done when a child is misbehaving. For example, your child is not sharing a toy nicely with his friend. Your limited choice in a discipline situation should include **one choice that describes the behaviour you want to see and one that will describe what will happen if the unacceptable behaviour *doesn't* stop.** An appropriate statement in the above example would be, "Michael, you have a choice. You can take turns using the toy with your friend, or I take the toy away for the day. What is your choice?" Be sure to wait for a definite choice and then proceed based on that.

It is important to realize that sometimes they will choose the more negative option. In this case, Michael might just say, "Take it away." You absolutely must follow through on this. It shows respect and that you do what you say you will do. This scenario tends to happen in the first few months of school for me; the students test me to see how I will react. If a child is talking too much while others are trying to work I usually warn them once and if they continue I use the choice question. "Karen, you can stay in the classroom and work without talking or you can take your books to the back desk and work there for 10 minutes. What is your choice?" Most often, they don't like having to work at the back desk so they choose to stop talking, but every so often, a student will choose to go back there. I act no differently when they make this choice. I simply say, "Okay, I'll invite you back in 10 minutes." At the beginning of the year my students are shocked that I don't get mad at them for choosing this, but after a few weeks or a couple of months, they actually will come and ask me if they can work at the desk for a while because they are having a hard time concentrating. They truly appreciate and respect the fact that I allow them to make their own choices.

Trick #4 – Take action...if need be

Research and my experience shows that children learn by direct experience, in other words, action. For this reason, Permissive Discipline doesn't work. All that talking, reasoning and lecturing doesn't accomplish anything. When you really see change in behaviour is when the child experiences a consequence.

Example: Your child has left her toys on the floor instead of cleaning up after herself. You tell her, "Hayley, clean up your toys. You need to put them away after you are done playing with them." She continues to leave her toys strewn around the next day so you say, "Haley, I spoke to you yesterday about leaving toys on the floor. You need to organize them each and every time you are finished playing with them. You have a choice. You can clean up after yourself, or you can leave them. If you leave them, just know that I will take them away for a week." What do you choose to do?" She says, "Clean up". She follows through with her choice for a couple of days, but later in the week you see those toys again. You take them and put them away as promised. When you see Hayley next, you explain that you've had to take them away and that she will get them back in a week. Hayley feels very bored for a week and begs you to give them back. She promises she'll put them away. You tell her that she can prove that to you after the week is over. Hayley always puts her toys back after this incident.

Some parents might say, "Why not just force her to put the toys away right then and there and give her a spanking?" What does this teach? The child learns to be fearful, feels embarrassed, and could tend to be resentful or revengeful towards you. In the above example, the child might be angry with you, but they will learn responsibility and a sense of being capable—this is what we are aiming for.

Now you know my four "Tricks of the Trade". These work every time. In almost all situations, I describe the behaviour I want, use my normal, matter of fact voice, give limited choices and take action if need be. Actually, I use these tricks so much that they come automatically to me. After I returned from France I taught as a substitute teacher for a while. One day I ended up teaching a high school French class. The boys in there towered over me. Some of them thought it was their lucky day when they saw me as their substitute so they tried to fool around. I automatically switched to my "Tricks" and began giving them a warning, and later a limited choice question. After the words rolled off my tongue, I giggled to myself because there I was, a 5 ft. 3 inch young lady giving limited choices to a 6 ft. 2 high school teenager! It worked though. He chose to sit down and got his work done! I was a little surprised back then, but this wouldn't shock me today because I know that if used consistently, these methods work with anybody in any situation.

I want you to feel that same confidence that I feel. I want those words to roll off your tongue just like they do mine. The time has come for you to train. Are you ready?

LET THE TRAINING BEGIN!

I want you to repeat the following words, in sequence, **5** times.

Describe...Normal Voice...Choices...Consequence

Now, cover the words and repeat them **5 more** times.

Now I want you to write these words on a separate piece of paper, **5** times. Write them *exactly* as they appear above. Say the words out loud as you write them.

Below, I want you to write one sentence in quotation marks that illustrates a **describing** statement. Look back to the section where I described this if you need to.

Describe... _____

Now, write a different describing sentence. However, this time read it back to yourself in a **normal, matter of fact voice**.

Normal Voice... _____

Think now of a situation you have had recently where your child has misbehaved. Come up with a limited **choices** question.

Choices... _____

Look at your question. What kind of **consequence** did you say would happen if the behaviour didn't stop? Write what action you would take on the line below.

Consequence... _____

Okay, by now you are definitely familiar with the four "Tricks of the Trade". However, I doubt you feel 100% confident using them. Don't worry, that's what the next section is all about.

I am going to provide you with scenarios. Read the scenario and think about the four "Tricks". How would you describe the behaviour you want? What choices would you give? And what consequence would you follow through with? Of course, you would be speaking in your matter-of-fact-voice.

In each of these scenarios, let's pretend that the behaviour persists and you are obliged to follow through with action. Please keep in mind, that when you start using this technique with your children, you *will* have to follow through with action most of the time. This is because they will be testing you. Remember, this is absolutely natural. As time goes on though, more often than not, you will get the behaviour to stop right after you pose the choices question simply because they will know from past experience that you *will* do what you say you will do.

After you have decided what you would say and do in each situation, turn to pages 77 -80 to review a response I would have given to that situation. Please note that my answer is not the *correct* or *only* answer, it is only provided so that you get an idea if you are on the right track or not. For example, if your scenario was that your young child was throwing food on the floor and your **describing** statement was "Sweetie, you have to stop doing that", you would see that it does not correspond well with mine of, "Amanda, no. You need to eat nicely." There is a distinct difference between the two. Notice that I always use the child's name when I start. Never use a term of endearment when you are disciplining, it lacks firmness and insinuates that the child doesn't really need to stop the behaviour.

Now, in all these scenarios the children don't stop the behaviour so you have to state your **choices** question. If yours is, "Please stop or else you will have to go to time out", you are doing alright. However when you read my response, you will notice and learn that you probably should cut out the "nicey nice" words and simply stick to basic, no nonsense language such as, "Amanda, you can eat nicely and stay with us here at the table, or you can go sit in time out for 5 minutes."

The scenario continues with Amanda waiting for you to look away and then testing you by throwing a little piece of potato on the floor and giggling. Let's say your decision after reading this scenario was to say nothing but pick the child up and take her to the time out room and let her stay there for 5 minutes. After the time lapsed you thought you would invite her back using a normal voice. This is very good. It coincides nicely with what my reaction would be ... "I would pick up Amanda and sit her in the time out chair and leave her there for 5 minutes. When 5 minutes is finished, I would walk over and say, 'You can come eat nicely now' in a matter-of-fact voice. If Amanda ate nicely I would show some form of physical contact such as putting my hand on hers and giving a loving squeeze or tap." You might learn a few extra things from my answer such as the physical contact I said I would initiate after Amanda behaved, but in general, you could feel confident that you were on the right track.

Before you begin I want to share a little tidbit with you. When I was trying to figure out the easiest way of describing how I decide on the consequence, I noticed a pattern. The pattern showed that when the situation involved an object, the consequence was to take the object away. When privileges were involved, the consequence was to take the privilege, such as watching TV, away for a period of time. Makes sense, doesn't it? But somehow, in the heat of the moment, it's easy to get lost in all the details, so that by the time you want to state your **choices** question, you don't quite know what to say. Below shows you how to pick out what is causing the problem and then how to take that cause out of the situation. It's common sense really, but I think it helps to see it laid out this way; it's easier to remember.

Easy Rules for Consequences

<u>Cause</u>	<u>Consequence</u>
Object	Take the object away for a period of time (Toy, fork being used inappropriately at the table)
Activity	Stop the activity for a period of time (Game)
Person	Remove from person for a while (Playmate, sibling)
Privilege	Take privilege away for a period of time (Playing Nintendo, time with friends)

Alright, this bit of information should make the training section easier. The steps are the same, **describe, normal voice, choices,** and **consequence,** only now, when you state your **choices** question, you won't have to stop for 30 seconds to decide what you should say, you'll just choose the consequence that matches the cause. Okay, here we go! Keep in mind that the first few might seem difficult but after the fifth one, you will be a pro!

Scenario One

Brian, 10 years old and David, his younger brother, are arguing over which Nintendo game to play. You begin to hear pushing and eventually slaps. What will you do?

Scenario Two

Your 13 year old daughter, Kristy, tells you she is going to her friend's house. She says she will be back in time for supper at 6:00 o'clock. You and the rest of your family begin eating dinner at 6:00pm, but Kristy is not home yet. You decide to wait another 30 minutes before you call her friend's house. At 6:30pm Kristy rushes in huffing and puffing saying, "Sorry, we got carried away talking and I totally lost track of the time!"

_____

_____

_____

_____

_____

_____

_____

_____

_____

_____

_____

_____

_____

_____

_____

_____

_____

_____

_____

_____

_____

_____

_____

Scenario Three

Daniel, your 16 year old son, is up in his bedroom and has his stereo turned up so loud that you can hear it downstairs. You are trying to read a book and are finding the noise to be overbearing. You go up to his room and ask him to turn it down because you are not able to enjoy your book downstairs. He reluctantly turns it down a little but not enough for your liking. What will you do?

_____

_____

_____

_____

_____

_____

_____

_____

_____

_____

_____

_____

_____

_____

_____

_____

_____

_____

_____

_____

_____

_____

_____

_____

_____

_____

_____

Scenario Four

Christopher has been forgetting his backpack on and off for a few weeks. Today, when his teacher asked him for his homework, he realized he had forgotten it again. If he doesn't hand his homework in today, he gets 10% off. He calls you at work and says, "I forgot my backpack again. If I don't hand my assignment in today, I will get 10% taken off. You need to bring it here at lunch!" What will you do?

_____

_____

_____

_____

_____

_____

_____

_____

_____

_____

_____

_____

_____

_____

_____

_____

_____

_____

_____

_____

_____

_____

_____

_____

Scenario Five

Carolina's bedroom is a catastrophe. There are clothes all over, dirty dishes on her desk and you could write your name in the dust on her dresser. You know she has plans to go to a sleepover at her friend's house tonight. What will you do?

_____

_____

_____

_____

_____

_____

_____

_____

_____

_____

_____

_____

_____

_____

_____

_____

_____

_____

_____

_____

_____

_____

_____

_____

_____

_____

_____

_____

CONGRATULATIONS! You have finished the most important part of the training. I would like you to take a few minutes to reflect on this exercise.

Did you notice your past discipline style wanting to come out?

Did you forget one of the steps regularly?

Did you find one of the steps most difficult to apply?

Did you find it difficult to pick out the cause of the problem but once you read my answers you understood better how to pick?

Answer these questions or make any other comments below.

_____
_____
_____
_____
_____
_____
_____
_____
_____
_____
_____
_____
_____
_____
_____
_____
_____
_____
_____
_____
_____
_____

Now that you have been trained and feel more comfortable using the 4 tricks, I want to give you another tip. The majority of the time you want to use the tricks exactly as I have trained, however, there are situations that arise where an even simpler version of my tricks can be used. Yes, I know it's hard to believe! You see, there are times when even less talking is okay.

Let's look at an example. You are talking on the telephone and your child starts whining for your attention. You can use my tricks as you have been trained or you can do this: Say, "You need to be patient and wait until I'm off the phone." If the whining continues and you need to deal with this quickly you say, "That's twice" or, once your child gets used to this fast track method, you can simply hold up two fingers. In essence, this second warning is their choice – decide to be patient or time out is on its way.

I use this quicker method when I'm not feeling very patient, when I'm stressed, or really focusing on something else. Why? In these circumstances my mind is less clear and I find it difficult to state my choices question without raising the tone of my voice. Why not just use this method all the time? One, because I believe children need to feel that they are being given a choice and if you state their choices clearly they feel like they are being respected. Two, they take responsibility for their actions because they begin to see the effects of their choices. And three, some situations are more complicated; like the scenarios given in the training section. If your daughter is coming home late all the time and you describe what she needs to do, then, if the next time she does it you say, "That's twice", it just isn't going to work. Use this fast track method in simple situations. These could be:

- You are talking on the telephone
- You are busy and very focused on something
- You are speaking to someone important

I think you get the picture. This fast track method is really handy in times when you are engaged in something and don't have the time or inclination to formulate a choices statement.

So, the fast track method looks like this:

Describe...Normal Voice...Count...Consequence

Or more specifically:

Describe...Normal Voice..."That's twice" ...Consequence

Don't worry that your child will get confused. The steps are in the same order and if they continue their behaviour the outcome is the same; this is all the consistency they need.

HOW TO PROCEED

Many of you might feel fully prepared to begin using these techniques right away and some of you may be thinking, "That's it? I don't feel ready!" Or maybe you are thinking there has to be more to this – how can disciplining be this simplistic?

For those of you who feel ready, I urge you to reread Chapter 2 again. Don't forget that our ingrained patterns are sometimes difficult to break, so just to be sure, read over the tricks again and be POSITIVE you are ready to begin implementing them. I also suggest sitting down with your partner and brainstorming common problems that you have already had to deal with. Practise using the tricks together. You could even role-play with one of you being your child and the other being the parent. Being a team is vitally important. You must agree that both of you will be consistent in using these techniques. It is not fair for one person to resort to their leniency or authoritative tendencies. Remember, the goal in all of this is to raise happy, self-sufficient, self confident, problem solving, and respectful children. These are the type of individuals our societies need. You have been given the responsibility to do this. Do not take this lightly, it's a major responsibility. Just think, if you use these techniques on a consistent basis, you will be gaining more quality time with your family! Instead of arguing, you'll all have more time to create positive, truly meaningful memories together.

For those of you feeling like you need more practise, I advise you to do the same activity as mentioned above. Practise in private, where you and your partner can fully open up to this experience. Perhaps you can do this activity just before bed, or maybe while your children are at a friend's house, or soccer practise. Practise until you and your partner both feel the words roll off your tongue.

Now, the first step to implementing these tricks is to have a family meeting. Call your family to the living room or dinner table and explain that some things are going to change in your household. Be serious with this conversation, but not serious in a discipline sort of way. This should be an informative conversation; stating what you and your partner have been noticing and what steps you are going to take to change these things. (*I highly suggest you read the entire book before doing this since there are some excellent ideas in Chapter 3 in regards to being proactive with common problems like shopping for groceries. This way you can address all relevant issues during this discussion. It won't be as effective if you call another meeting and say, "Oh yeah, and one more thing..."*

I do a talk like this at the beginning of each school year. I tell the students to gather in the library of our classroom for a class meeting. I start by telling them that in order for a classroom to run smoothly a few guidelines must be put into place. I state that I think it's only fair to describe to them how I work as a teacher in the event that someone chooses not to follow our classroom guidelines. I then provide them with an example. It goes something like this.

"Let's say I have asked the class to work on a Math problem and a girl named Becky begins chatting with the person behind her. I will start by saying, 'Becky, you need to turn around and focus on the Math problem.' Sounds simple, right? Most times when I ask nicely students turn around and respectfully focus on what they need to, however there may be times when that student might have something else on their mind and I'll need to remind them again. I might say, 'Becky, I have asked you nicely to turn around already. You can stay at your desk and work on the problem, or you can go work at the back desk to help you concentrate. What's your choice?'

At this point, I usually ask the students, "What do you think Becky would do?" Many think they are giving the correct answer if they say, 'She turned around.' I then ask them, "Would it be bad if she chose to go to the back desk?" Some still say yes, but others figure out that it wouldn't be by my tone. I then explain to the students that my whole goal is to get Becky to stop talking so that her classmates can concentrate better. If Becky thinks moving away for a while will help her, then why not? I love watching the kids' faces at this point. They think this is pretty cool. Immediately they feel comfortable in this classroom and with me. I review with them the three steps. 1) A warning 2) Asked to make a choice 3) If the behaviour continues they are now making a conscious choice to be rude and will be asked to work at the desk until invited back. They LOVE this! I often smile to myself throughout the year when I hear another teacher discipline a student of mine and I hear the student say in all seriousness, "But you didn't give me a warning." Children feel safe and comfortable when they know what is expected of them and what will happen if they mess up. If a consequence is handed out, they will not argue or feel revengeful, they will simply learn from the experience and have time to think about what is appropriate and what isn't.

Use this example as a guide to your own family meeting. Bring up important issues for YOUR family. Maybe there are certain jobs you want them to help with, maybe the tone in which everyone has been speaking must change. In any case, give them particular examples and state what series of statements they can expect from you and your partner from now on. Take them to the spot you have designated as time out and explain to them that this will be the place they will go to think about the inappropriate behaviour that occurred. Be sure to tell them that the amount of time will be associated with their age. Explain that as you get older it takes longer for a person to calm down. Give an example from your life. If you are 34, tell them that this is why you sometimes tell them you need a half an hour rest. In addition to this, I strongly encourage you to brainstorm a family tradition that your family would like to begin (See Chapter 4 for ideas). It is important for the meeting to have a bonding component to it as well so that it doesn't come off as negative. Your children must see that you and your partner have been giving the family dynamics real thought. Your goal is to create a happier, more solid family unit. To conclude the meeting have all children repeat the statements you will be using along with you, then congratulate them and mention that you and your partner are very excited about the changes that are in store for your family.

Summary

The feelings you experienced as you went through each scenario is pretty much how your child will feel once you begin using the four "Tricks of the Trade" with them. They will at times feel frustrated, confused, self-confident, self-assured, angry, happy and content. Be patient with yourself, but if you know you messed up, come back to the training section again to refresh your memory and confidence. Your children will test you, this is for sure. However, the more they experience action and not just empty words, the more they will understand that you do what you say you will do.

The time it takes for a child to accept this style of discipline is different for each youngster. Sometimes I have used it once and they learn. With my worst case I had to use it for 2 or 3 months before they fully understood. But trust me; they will turn around if you are consistent. They eventually get tired of experiencing the consequences so they make better choices. Sometimes, a child can be very well behaved for 6 months straight but because of hormones, peer pressure, or struggles at school they begin testing you. This is not the time to back down and feel sorry for them, this is the time they really need to feel safe, and that comes from an inner sense of knowing what you will do if they act a certain way... you will apply consequences. It seems like a very strange phenomenon, but I assure you that this is how children's minds work.

Being a teacher, I hear more about parents and how their children feel about them than parents themselves hear. Let me share three quick stories with you in order to prove just how much children actually crave and thrive on discipline.

I was teaching French as a Second Language class one day and we were studying language around the topic of television. We were learning how to say what program was their favourite and explaining why it was their favourite. When I gave an assignment to watch one particular show, a boy raised his hand and said proudly, "My mom doesn't allow me to watch TV during the week." The class was stunned. He answered their questions with this beautiful statement, "She says school is more important than TV and now we actually play more games together as a family. It's cool you guys!" After this, a few boys said things like, "My mom lets me watch whatever I want, she's doesn't care," and "Yeah, I get home and watch TV from 3:30 until almost bedtime while my parents drink and smoke." This last little boy began acting out how his father sat in the chair and slurred words and everyone laughed but I knew what both boys were really telling us. They were expressing their unhappiness with their situation. I could see they just wished their parents paid more attention to them by setting boundaries.

One other time a boy in my class who was usually a very studious student began handing in work that was below average and his test marks were dropping rapidly. I send a weekly folder home to parents to show the assignments or tests that we have completed that week along with comments and their child's grades. When this boy came back on Monday, he handed me his folder and said, "You know what? My parents were so unhappy with my grades they grounded me for this whole week. I have to show them I can improve." He was trying to complain but he could barely stop smiling! It was the funniest thing. Here he was, grounded for the whole week and he wasn't thrilled about it, but I could see his comfort in how interested his parents were about his school work.

Another situation was when I was talking to two little girls at recess and they brought up how hard it was going through their parents' divorces. We talked about their feelings and then one of the little girls said, "I'm actually happier now though because my mom is the only one disciplining me and she doesn't let me do anything else until I finish my homework. And, every time I come home with good grades and comments in my weekly folder, I get a smiley face on a chart. If I get 2 weeks in a row with all smiley faces, I get to do something really special with my mom." Her face was glowing while she talked and I could feel her comfort in this and the self-confidence she displayed. This was a huge change because I was getting quite concerned in earlier months that she was falling behind rapidly due to family stress. The mother really took hold of the situation and all her children benefited. It was truly beautiful to see.

These are just three stories. I could share thousands of stories just like them. Children need you to be their trainer. And, even though they test you, it does not mean they don't love you or respect you. It means they aren't finished their research as to how this whole world works.

I sincerely congratulate you for working through the exercises patiently. You will be giving your child the biggest gift you could ever give them. Go ahead now and start using the techniques with your children. Sit them down first and discuss that things are going to be a bit different. Tell them that you are going to ask them once nicely to do something. If they choose not to do it they will be asked to make a choice. If they decide to continue the behaviour, they are choosing to continue and will have to experience a consequence. It would be a good idea to give an example here so that they understand the meaning of the word consequence.

Remember that within a boundary there can be space as well. This space allows for choices and rights. Be sure to discuss some of the recent problems and ask them to help find solutions to these problems. Make this discussion important by listening attentively to their suggestions as to how to correct the problems; it will mean a lot to them. They will feel like a respected, valuable, member of the family.

My best wishes go out to you. I congratulate you for reading and participating in the activities presented in this section. Any parent who feels it's important enough to look for a book to help them is one who has great courage. Move forward now and be the great parent that you are!

Chapter Three

WARDING OFF COMMON PROBLEMS

I am adding this section because I believe proactive measures are "the best" way of minimizing or avoiding conflicts. When I plan my lessons as a teacher, I am always thinking about any proactive measures I can use to avoid "trouble". For example, when I know I will be asking the students to get into groups, I am aware that there are some children who work well together and others that don't. I also plan the size of the groups based on what needs to be accomplished in the activity. In addition to this, I arrange my seating plan to suit the many different styled learners I may have. I have also set up a "Job Station" in the classroom so that a) our classroom stays tidy and b) the students learn responsibility.

While reflecting on my experiences in teaching as well as taking care of three boys in France, I realized that there were certain problems that continuously arose where distinct guidelines were needed. When comparing my experiences with other mothers and fathers, my belief was solidified; there were common problems among most families that needed clear guidelines for children to follow. This chapter reviews those problems and suggests ways to be proactive.

HOMEWORK

As a teacher, I've heard every excuse in the book for homework not being done or why it's at home. The only time I have seen and felt real success with students consistently forgetting their homework or not having it done, was when the parents, child and I sat down together and reviewed the ground rules for homework. Here's how a good system works.

Look at your family's weekly schedule.

-   What time does your child/children get home from school?
-   At what time could you consistently eat dinner on the week-days?
-   What time will one parent be available to be home while the child is doing the homework?
-   What after dinner jobs must be completed by your child/children? Ex. Clear dishes, load dishwasher, wash/dry dishes, sweep the floor?
-   Where is a good location for your child/children to do their homework? They should have a comfortable chair, a clear space to work on, the room should be quiet without distractions and all necessary materials such as pens, pencils, erasers and rulers should be present.

Now that you have answered these important questions, here is an example of how one family answered these questions and how they arranged their child's homework schedule.

Linda works for an insurance company and Mark works for an IT consulting company. Their children arrive home from school at 3:45pm, Linda arrives home at 5:00pm, and Mark arrives home at 5:30pm. They have two children and they said that each child has a desk in their room. They agreed that they usually eat supper between 6:00pm and 6:30pm. Jobs that were expected from the boys after supper were to clear their plates from the table and put them in the dishwasher. Linda and Mark said the time they would be available to help with homework was after all the dishes were done, at approximately 7:30pm.

I asked Linda and Mark if there was any way one of them could start work earlier in the morning and leave earlier in the afternoon. Mark said his job could be flexible with that. Therefore, this is the plan we came up with.

3:45 Boys arrive home, have a nutritious snack, read a magazine or chat. No TV!
4:15 Begin homework. They have until 6:00pm to finish everything, no later! (See explanation below)
4:30 Mark arrives home, says hi to the boys, does work of his own, reads, or begins dinner, but is available to the boys in case they have a question.

When the children are finished their homework they will call Mark and he will check to see if everything is completed and done neatly. After a few weeks of acceptable completion, Mark can check periodically or until the teacher sends a note saying, "Work isn't being completed."

5:00 Linda arrives home and begins or helps to make dinner.
6:00 Dinner time – family eats and shares stories about the day (see chapter on Family Traditions for helpful information on meal times)
6:45 Everyone clears their plate from the table, puts them in the dishwasher and then the boys are free to play at a friends house, watch TV, read, play a game, or watch a movie.
8:45 Boys change into their pyjamas and brush their teeth, go to sleep or read in bed.
9:15 Lights out.

What happens if their homework is not completed by 6:00pm? Basically, you use the "tricks", and if need be, follow through with a consequence of all privileges being taken away for that night. If the homework is something that can be finished in an hour or less, the child should finish the homework that night then have "quiet time" where they are only allowed to do something quiet like reading. If the assignment that wasn't completed is something large like a report or story, write a note to the teacher that your child will work on it the following night and will hand it in the next day and will face any consequences the teacher sees fit. Obviously, if the behaviour persists, you will need to extend the removal of privileges for a week.

Communication between you, your child, and your child's teacher is imperative. The following information should be discussed at a family meeting before the first school day of the year. The teachers only, and I mean ONLY job is to be the assignment giver and grader, not the homework monitor. Your job as parent should only be to provide a comfortable, quiet and organized work space for your child. Your job is NOT and I do repeat NOT to be your child's homework monitor. At first, yes, you will have to do a bit of monitoring, however, your goal is to quickly refrain from this. After your child has realized that homework is THEIR responsibility and that they will NOT be experiencing privileges until after their homework is finished, you can sit back and feel comfortable knowing that you have provided all you need to…the rest is up to the child.

I can guarantee that if you are having difficulties with your child not completing homework now, things will get worse before they get better. You just have to keep reminding yourself, "If I stay consistent, then this whole process will be over sooner and I won't ever have these struggles again." I cannot emphasize enough that if you are inconsistent even once, you have set yourself back another 1-2 weeks. It definitely pays to stay consistent from the beginning.

How do you stay strong? Well, this is the good part. You have extremely good leverage if you use my homework plan. Think about it. Children have more energy in the day therefore it only makes sense to have them complete the work *before* they experience free time. It's a goal for them; they become *more* energized when they know that there is something good at the end of it.

If you allow your child to do his/her homework after dinner, think about how your night would be ruled by your child's homework. You wouldn't have any down time until they went to bed and by that time you would be too exhausted to do anything but go to bed yourself! I know many, many parents who have this type of homework routine and

I'll tell you, it isn't working for them. What leverage do these parents have? None! After dinner, most kids will complain, whine that they are too tired, or that their "ultimate favourite show is on." The only leverage the parents have now is that if their children don't do their homework tonight, they won't be able to play with their friends tomorrow. I know kids very well and parents saying this won't bother them in the least. In fact, I'm almost positive that the child's first response will be, "Okay." What's the problem with this? The problem is that nine times out of ten the parents end up having the same discussion the next day. Only immediate consequences work. Saying that tomorrow a consequence will be applied is just fine with the child because it's too far away for them to realize what they will feel like tomorrow. Plus, if you use this method, you have taught them that all they need to do is whine enough and you will change your mind or just give up.

Summary

You need to sit down and write a schedule that fits your lifestyle, keeping in mind of course that homework must be completed before dinner time. Make this work. Rearrange things, cut out needless after school commitments, do what you have to do to make this work. Your next move is to sit down with your child and present the schedule to them. Be sure you also review the consequences of what will happen if they do not finish their homework before dinner time. (Remember, the odd time they might have a longer project they need to finish up, but this should not have to interfere with the weekday schedule too much.) Next, set up a meeting with your child's teacher and have your child present the schedule to his or her teacher; this makes them accountable. The only thing left to do is to stick to the schedule 100%. Especially at the beginning, it is imperative for you to apply consequences if your child does not comply. And remember, it is almost guaranteed that they won't comply for the first little while because they are testing you to see just how serious you are about this. Be strong, smile inside, and apply the consequence!

Don't forget the "Tricks of the Trade!"...**Describe... Normal Voice... Choices...Consequence**

ALLOWANCES

I used to believe that giving rewards was a good thing for children. It showed you were proud of their efforts and they were left feeling excited and happy with themselves. I soon realized though that my students were beginning to ask, "What do we get if we do that?" I would become perturbed that they would ask this and reply, "You don't just do things to get something. You do it because you are being a kind person." However, the next day, I was handing out chocolate money to those people who did their weekly jobs well. Hmmm... something was wrong here. If I wanted my students to learn to do things from their hearts or because they had learned how to be responsible, why was I at times providing rewards for their actions? No wonder they were confused! As well, some boys stopped caring about the darn chocolates and therefore stopped doing their jobs! After I made this realization, I totally revised my thinking and actions the following year. What I witnessed were students learning how to be responsible, generous, and self-confident. Jobs were being done because they knew they were expected to be done and not because they'd get a chocolate. Kids were writing letters to the janitor thanking him for keeping their classroom so clean, and now all I saw on the students' faces after getting a thumbs up from me was pride.

I share this story with you because I know allowances are an issue with today's parents. Kids want to do more and have more as do most adults. It is becoming increasingly difficult to keep up with buying new clothes, shoes, school supplies and entertainment than ever before! I will share a couple of ideas with you regarding allowances. These are ones I agree with and have seen work for a variety of families. They teach kids how to manage money and feel the pride of saving and buying something for themselves by themselves.

1) Every week, no questions asked, your child gets $5.00-$20.00 depending on what you can afford. However, the trick is, this is the only money they get from you for entertainment or extras they want. You do not attach this money to chores or behaviour that week. This is something they know they will receive no

matter what. Doing this will help maintain the feeling of trust and respect between you and your child. Even if you have had a bad week with them, hand them their allowance without comments like, "Here you go...even though you don't deserve it." These kinds of comments are like ones a punitive parent would give. Remember, we are trying to build our children up, not make them feel like they are bad people. Plus, in the real world, when we are grumpy or have a few bad days does our boss say, "You don't get paid this week"? No. Therefore, let's keep allowances a positive, real life experience for them.

What happens if your child really wants something and they don't have enough money to buy it? Well, explain to them when you set up this allowance routine that they have an option of performing extra duties in order to earn more money. These jobs must be explained and even written down fully so that they don't do the job half way and then expect payment. As well, each job must have an amount attached to them so that you aren't haggling over how much you owe them. Be detailed about how you expect each job to be done then they cannot argue. For example, an extra job might be to cut the grass if the child is older and they will receive 10 or 15 dollars if they do it according to your description. For younger children, they might rake leaves or prepare their own school lunch. (See a list of tasks in the "Chores/Teamwork Tasks" section of this chapter for further ideas.)

2) Every week, no questions asked, you give your child $5 - $20 depending on your financial situation or age of your children and then they record this amount into a cheque book under "credit". When they buy things they must save their receipt and deduct the money they spent in the debit column. Once a month you go through their check book with them to see if it all balances. This is a great Math lesson and they will see their patterns of spending. You can even talk to them about how they felt this month and what they might continue doing or change next month.

Summary

Allowances can be one of the best ways to maintain or instigate a connection between you and your child. They will feel that you love and respect them even when they have had a bad week; there's no guilt trip. As well, your child will feel pride and his or her self esteem will grow. Any child that has a healthy self esteem will have fewer problems respecting authority. Pick which system fits you best, prepare all necessary charts or descriptions of extra jobs and money attached to them, then sit down with your child and review how allowances will work from now on. Watch your child's facial expressions and body language when they make their first purchase and all this will feel so right to you.

GROCERY SHOPPING

This topic is one where pre-planning works like a charm to avoid hassles and frustration. I will list a few proactive things you can do so that this experience is enjoyable for you *and* your child.

1) Plan meals for approximately one month and if applicable in your country, shop on Customer Appreciation Day where you save between 10-15% off of your total bill. (In Canada it's usually the first Tuesday of each month) Include your children's ideas in this too. For example, tell them to choose five meals for the month. Then, on the weekend before Customer Appreciation Day, sit down with recipe books and pick recipes that interest you or that you know are all time favourites. You can even write down Pizza Night or Chinese Night to remind you to order in on a night when you are too tired to cook. Write down all the ingredients you will need on one sheet of paper and write the name of the recipe, name of the book and the page number on a separate sheet. (I usually use a fridge magnetic pad for this) Now, when you go to the grocery store, you have a list to prevent you from overspending and you save 10-15%! While shopping, hand the list over to your children and have them call out the items and cross them off once you've gotten them. This will give your child something to do and keep their mind focused instead of just having to tag along with you for an hour. I do this every month and I find it saves me the stress of trying to figure out what to cook each night and wondering if I have all the ingredients. The savings is pretty nice too!

2) Be sure to have a snack in your purse in case hunger strikes one of your children. You never know what they'll ask for if they're hungry!

3) Before leaving the house, **describe** your expectations of behaviour for them. (Only do this if you have been having a lot of problems with tantrums, whining, etc.) If your child begins having a tantrum or whining, give the **choices** question, and if need be, follow through with a **consequence.** For example: Your daughter is whining and begging for toys she sees along

the aisles. Stop the cart, look into her eyes and say in a **normal** but firm **voice**, "Jillian, you need to stop whining." If the whining continues say, "If you continue, we will go to the car and wait until you have calmed down and can act appropriately. You have a choice. You can stay here and finish shopping nicely or we can go to the car and wait for you to be ready to shop nicely. What is your choice?" If she calms down, carry on. If she persists, drive the cart to the customer service area and ask them if you can leave the cart there for a few minutes. Then, head out to the car and wait. This is not easy and you will feel like exploding at times. However, remember that if you go out to that car, she will know you mean business and this will help her understand that whining does not work with you. The next time you go grocery shopping, she might start whining to test you, but as soon as you put that choice to her again, she will remember quickly that whining doesn't work. In other words, do it once or twice rather than 20 or more times.

4)   A great idea I heard from one mother was to give your toddler a short list of easy to find ingredients like eggs, milk, or apples. She tried to ensure that there was an item from the beginning, middle, and end of her shopping route. She would constantly say, "Have you seen anything yet?" or "Keep an eye out for those eggs". This way your child will feel important and part of the shopping routine.

Summary

Save time, money, and frustration by being prepared. The worst thing you could do is bring hungry children to the grocery store and walk up and down the aisles aimlessly searching for dinner ideas. Ask your local grocery store when their customer appreciation day is and then sit down with your beautiful, inspirational cookbooks a night or two before the big day. Be sure to thoroughly scan the recipe for any necessary ingredients or baking pans and write these down on one notepad. Have another notepad for the title of the recipe, page number and name of the cookbook. I suggest researching at least 10-15 meals. Let the rest of the days be for leftovers, quicker, healthy frozen foods, or dining out. Depending on the age of your child, get them involved in an appropriate way. Younger toddlers can have their own list with pictures (cut pictures from flyers) and older children can be sent off to find certain items which you then cross off your list. Always have a snack in your purse so that if you or your children are hungry you can solve that problem right away.

DINING OUT/RESTAURANTS

I was walking into a restaurant the other day and saw a father with his 2-3 year old son carrying a take-out container. I overheard the father say, "See how nice the restaurant is? When you are able to handle being in a restaurant we can actually eat in there instead of taking the food home."

At first I thought how cute that was, and how good it was of the father to be explaining this to his son, then I thought to myself, "Hey, wait a minute. Shouldn't they be able to eat out already? If they had been taking him to restaurants since he was a baby, wouldn't the boy feel comfortable enough there?"

Although it might not be the *most* enjoyable experience to eat in a restaurant with a two year old, it is doable if some proactive methods have taken place. First, you teach your children how to eat at home. If you train your child at home and expect good manners always, they will handle a restaurant experience with ease. If on the other hand you allow your child to scream, sit incorrectly, burp, and talk with his/her mouth full at home, then do not expect a well-behaved child at a restaurant. Just because *you* know certain behaviours are expected at restaurants doesn't mean they do. Remember, *you* are the trainer. Your children look to you to see how these things are done. Why not plan a special family dinner once- a - month, where your children help decide on the menu and all the special dishes, glasses and silverware are used. This would be the perfect time to teach and have them practise good manners and dinner etiquette. (See chapter on Family Traditions for more ideas).

Everyone has their own level of expectations at a restaurant, however, I would like to suggest a few that should be the bare minimum.

1) Stay seated at the table – no running around the restaurant.
2) If the washroom is required, whisper in mom or dad's ear – no yelling.
3) Use the words 'please' and 'thank you'
4) When ordering, use phrases like, "I will have..." or "I would like ..."

So, training begins at home. If you make plans to visit a restaurant, sit down and have a chat before leaving or better yet, the night before during dinner. Review and practise your expectations. Have fun with this; it doesn't need to be extremely serious. Pretend you are the waiter or waitress and have them respond. Congratulate them and say, "I knew you would be able to handle this well. I'm so excited to go there with you tomorrow night!"

If your child is younger, bring along small toys, a portable DVD player or colouring books for them to play with while you and your partner have "talk time". Train them for this as well. Practise at home and re-mind them that this is what he/she will be doing at the restaurant.

For older children, train them to add interesting comments to adult discussions. As well, while in an adult conversation, try to include your child by saying things like, "Andrea, didn't your teacher talk to your class about conservation last week? What was she saying again?" On the car ride home, always talk about the evening. Mention how nice it was when they added a certain comment, or how proud you were of them when they did this or that, etc. This is a great way to reinforce the behaviour you expect.

Now, I can hear the questions running through your mind. What if we trained them, but they act inappropriately? Well, you will be pleased to know that time-outs *are* possible at a restaurant. First, in your nor-mal, **matter-of-fact voice**, you **describe** the behaviour you spoke about earlier, and what you expect of them now. If they continue, you provide them with a **choice**. Something like, "You can sit properly here like I've asked, or I can take you to the car for a time-out. What is your choice?" If they continue, then you take their hand firmly and walk out to the car without saying anything. Do not engage in any discussion whatsoever. They might be screaming, but you just deep breathe and stay focused remembering that if you do it right this time, you won't have many, if any, reoccurrences later. Depending on the child's age (1 minute for every year old) have them sit in the car. After the time elapses, turn to them and say, "Are you ready to go inside and act how we discussed?" If they say "yes" properly, say "Thank you" and move on. If they respond in a really snarky tone, ask them to repeat what they said in a more appropriate way. If they do, thank them. If they don't, say, "I guess you need a little more time to relax in here" and wait the same number of minutes as before. Repeat until the desired behaviour is achieved. Once they have agreed to act appropriately I would make this a big deal by saying, "That's the way. I knew you could say that nicely. Let's go finish our yummy meal."

One other trick is to carry a light snack in your purse in case an unexpectedly long wait occurs. I know how grumpy I get when I'm hungry – why would we expect anything else from a child?

Summary

Training is the most important factor in deciding whether or not you have an enjoyable experience at a restaurant with your family. Be clear about your expectations and practise them at your own home. You might not mind having the noise level a bit higher during dinner at home, but you will still expect to hear the words, 'please' and 'thank you', for example. If your child chooses to act inappropriately at a restaurant then begin using the four "Tricks of the Trade". Remember that time-outs *do* work in this case. You simply take your child to the car for the time-out period. Always use the car ride home to congratulate, praise or simply thank your child or children for such an enjoyable evening. Be specific when praising them. For example, "You really sat nicely at the restaurant. Mom and Dad had a great time with you tonight."

CHORES A.K.A TEAMWORK TASKS

One of the best ways to teach responsibility, teamwork, and being a valuable contributor is to assign chores. Children love to feel they are part of something special. If you make your children feel like they are helping the family team then they will be more receptive to helping out. I do this at school as well. I have a large sign saying Team Help Line. Underneath I have three strings with clothes pins on them. Each string represents a job. For example, Handout Helpers, Agenda Helpers, Tidy-Up Helpers. On the first day of school I hand them a pattern of a T-Shirt and ask them to write their name neatly on it. I then ask them to decorate their shirt. When everyone is finished, I hang two T-shirts on the Handout Helper Line, two on the Agenda Helper Line and two on the Tidy-Up Line. I go through my expectations for each job by listing them on the board, and modelling the actual job in action. They love this because I make it fun! I tell them that they are responsible for this job for the entire week. If someone notices their partner is not on top of things, they are allowed to gently remind them of their job. Each Monday their job will change. The pair that was on the top line goes to the second line, the pair that was on the second line goes to the third, and the pair that was on the third line gets taken off the board and a new pair takes their place on the top line. Throughout the week I compliment each pair periodically for doing a great job. I am always very specific with my praise. For example, "I noticed there were many pillows lying around our library before lunch. I want to thank our Tidying Helpers for noticing this too and cleaning up. Some parents were getting a tour of the school and I felt extremely proud to have them see our lovely classroom. Thanks, guys!" I always give a smile, wink, thumbs up, or quick tap on the back while saying something like this– it solidifies the compliment.

My goal as a teacher is to create a classroom community, to teach responsibility, accountability, and a sense of being a valuable contributor to the class community. These goals really aren't that different than the reasons many parents want to assign chores.

Where do you begin? At what age do you start introducing chores? What chores are appropriate for each age? How do I enforce the chores? These are many of the questions probably running through your mind right now. Let's begin by changing the word, "Chores" to "Teamwork Tasks". The word "chore" has such negative connotations that you are setting yourself up for resistance right away. You want to feel like your family is a team, don't you? You want to feel like everyone is doing their part to make it run efficiently. It feels good when you see everyone doing their part to make your home a nice place to come home to. Children feel a sense of pride as well knowing that your family is a team.

I remember witnessing this concept one day when there was a music festival in our city. Many students from the three grade 4 classes were singing in the choir at this festival. The other teachers accompanied the choir students whereas I stayed back at the school to look after the students not involved in the festival. I watched my students swell with pride, just by having others enter our classroom. The other students were looking around at all the things we had on the walls. My students proudly shared why each item was there or what a certain sign meant. One student in particular made me smile, because after he was finished sharing the ways our classroom runs with another student he said, "We have expectations in our classroom." With that said, he sat up straight, looking unbelievably proud and happy, and got right down to his work. Children really do love to feel part of a team that works together for a purpose. The other part of establishing this "team" feeling comes later in the chapter on family traditions.

The following ideas for Teamwork Tasks are ones suggested by many pediatric associations, and ones I've learned through my education and interaction with children and parents over the years, however, most of them come from my own particular upbringing. My parents had the philosophy from day one that their children were entering their family and that their children would need to help contribute to the family. I thank my parents for teaching and expecting these jobs to be done because even to this day, we feel like a team, and oh, what a great feeling that is.

Teamwork Tasks for Toddlers

1. Brush their teeth
2. Comb their hair
3. Climb in and out of the car seat

4. Feed themselves with fingers or a spoon
5. Help with grocery shopping (see section on Grocery Shopping)
6. Help put away groceries
7. Clean up toys by putting them in their place
8. Request one menu item for the monthly grocery list (see Grocery Shopping section)
9. Take their dishes to the dishwasher. You can decide if you want them to actually place the dish in the dishwasher)
10. Hang coat on their own hook and place shoes on shoe rack
11. Put clothes in hamper

Teamwork Tasks for 4 year olds

*same tasks as Toddlers. Simply add:
1. Help set the table
2. Suggest two menu items for the month
3. Feed pets
4. Dress themselves
5. Wash themselves (with supervision) in the bath
6. Make own bed
7. Vacuum crumbs in kitchen (with hand-held vacuum)
8. Make a choice between two outfits you have chosen for them.

Teamwork Tasks for 5 year olds

* same tasks as the younger ages. Add:
1. Choose their outfit for the day. You may want to help make suggestions on items that would work nicely together. Give a few choices stating particular reasons why each outfit looks good. For example, "It's warm outside, so a dress or skirt would be perfect for today." Or, "I like your choice. Blue shirts look really nice with brown pants."
2. Learn to tie shoes
3. Pull weeds from the garden or water trees and flowers. They love this!

Teamwork Tasks for 6 year olds

*same as younger ages. Add:
  1. Serve themselves at the dinner table
  2. Make a sandwich for their lunch. (With supervision)
  3. Keep bedroom tidy i.e. bed made, regularly dusted, toys organized
  4. Pour own drinks
  5. Tie own shoes
  6. Choose their outfit without supervision

Teamwork Tasks for 7 year olds

*same as younger ages. Add:
  1. Empty all household garbage cans and throw bag of refuse in large bin outside
  2. Answer telephone appropriately and take a message if need be
  3. Set the table for dinner
  4. Wash pets
  5. Use an alarm clock to wake self up for school

Teamwork Tasks for 8 and 9 year olds

*same as younger ages. Add:
  1. Take garbage or recycle bins to the curb
  2. Take dirty clothes in hamper to the laundry room
  3. Make own lunch with assistance in planning.
     *When I was young I used to make a lunch menu list for the week. I would show it to my mother to ask what she thought and then each day I would pack my lunch according to the list. This is not for everyone, but you might want to try introducing this.
  4. Help with simple household cleaning duties. Ex. Dusting, cleaning mirrors

Teamwork Tasks for 10 and 11 year olds

*same as younger ages. Add:
1. Load and run the dishwasher
2. Do seasonal jobs for neighbours such as raking leaves and shovelling snow
3. Help wash the car, both inside and out
4. Help with more difficult household duties. Ex. Vacuuming, cleaning bathrooms, shining the kitchen ie: wipe down cupboard fronts, wipe behind toasters, blenders, use a stainless steel cleaner on the sink

Teamwork Tasks for 12 year olds

*same as younger ages. Add:
1. Take responsibility for the changing of their sheets every two weeks or every month
2. Separate and wash loads of laundry without assistance
3. Baby-sit for younger siblings or neighbours' children
4. Earn money by mowing the lawn for the family or neighbours

As with most family issues, a family meeting is the best way to introduce the concept of Teamwork Tasks. State the reason for them, how, by everyone helping out, your family is a team that takes care of each other so not only one person gets stuck with all the work. Describe the pay-off. When the house is tidy, life runs more smoothly for everyone, it shows appreciation for what you have, etc. Ask them if they can think of a good reason to have Teamwork Tasks. Following this, you can show your children a list of Tasks and have them decide which ones they would like to be responsible for, or assign jobs based on their age. Another idea might be to show them this book with all the Tasks listed for each age, so it looks more official. Another area to discuss is *when* the Tasks will be completed. Do you want beds made first thing in the morning? Should the dishwasher be loaded immediately after dinner? It is vitally important to inform them that if the jobs are not completed correctly, or if they are not completed at all, they will have no TV, time with friends, or time on the phone until they are finished appropriately. You can use a sports team analogy here if you like. For example, "Can you imagine if everyone showed up for the hockey game except the goalie? Or, maybe the goalie showed up, but he didn't try his best for the team and they lost? This is how the rest of the family would feel if you didn't do your part, therefore, these tasks are expectations, not choices, because you are part of this family team."

After your children have been assigned Tasks, tell them that each Task has certain requirements in order to be called finished. Proceed to model what each job looks like and then ask them to try. Be specific here with your requirements and compliment them when you see them doing it correctly. Ask them if they have any questions, and then say something like, "This is going to be so much fun as a team! Go, Kurts!" (Of course, insert *your* family name here)

Don't think toddlers are too young for this. Young children actually *love* to help. If you start early, adding more Tasks as they get older, this whole process will be more natural since the routine is already established.

What do you think the routine would be if the Tasks were not finished as modelled or, not finished at all? Think about this for a minute before reading on. How would you handle this based on your knowledge of the four "Tricks of the Trade"?

If you said you would go to your child and **describe** what needs to be done in a **firm, matter of fact voice**, great job! If you thought further into the possibility that they still didn't complete the task after you described the behaviour and decided you would then go to them and give a **choices** question, you are amazing! And if you thought further still about the possibility your child refused to do the Task and that you would carry through with the **consequence**, well, now you are a pro. See how natural this all becomes?

Summary

Teamwork Tasks help in creating a smooth running, team-inspired household. Not only one person or the parents are responsible for the daily tasks, children are too. By involving them, your family will be bonded on a new level. Although there may be times when your children complain, you have to understand that the ultimate feeling, later on, will be one of thankfulness; thankfulness for teaching them how to take care of themselves when they're older, thankfulness for knowing what responsibility is, and thankfulness for making them feel like they were, and still are, part of the most important team they've ever been on.

Remember to have a family meeting to discuss what needs to be done and then model how it is to be done. Let your child try the task and use this time to be very specific – not critical, just specific. Your tone of voice will be important here. For example, if your child is cleaning the bathroom and thinks she's finished, say, "Things look great. You also need to remember to wipe the toilet paper holder. That's important, as it can get very dusty and sticky." Be sure to discuss when each task must be completed. Do you want them to hang up their coat and put away their shoes before they sit down for their after school snack? Do you want them to fill and run the dishwasher right after dinner is finished?

Finally, always remember that everyone likes a compliment when a job is well done. Don't you feel good when your boss acknowledges some work you did? There is no need to go over the top with this, or say things all the time, as your compliments will appear ungenuine. Simply choose to comment on something you actually saw and appreciated. Most importantly though is to concentrate on calling yourselves a team. Phrases like, "And we did it!" or "Now, doesn't our home look and feel great? Thanks, everyone", or "What a beautiful feeling it is to walk into this sparkling kitchen this morning." Get the picture?

BEDTIME

If you begin a bedtime routine when your children are young, prefer-
ably babies, you will have few if any problems putting your child to
bed at night. Start with a bath if you like then change them into their
pyjamas, have them brush their teeth, tuck them in with special objects
or stuffed animals, place a glass of water beside their bed depending on
their age, give a choice of three books and read one or two depending
on their length, give them a kiss, tell them how much you love them,
maybe have them say three things they are grateful for, you reply with
your three, and then lights out. This routine can begin up to an hour before the actual time you want lights out, but no longer. Be sure to keep
this time quiet, possibly having Mozart or other classical music playing
in the background. As your children grow older, get them involved in
the routine. You can say, "It's time to run your bath. Bring your pyjamas
to the bathroom, please."

What happens if you have a baby sitter putting them to bed, or you
have taken your child to a friend's house and plan to stay there well
after your child's bedtime? These are special circumstances and actually are quite good for your child to experience every once in a while.
Although routine is good, and makes children feel safe, they also need
to learn how to be flexible. Being flexible takes away anxiety, therefore
be sure to change the routine every once in a while. Too often, such as
weekly, is not a good idea, but once or twice a month is perfectly fine. If
the baby sitter is a family member whom you trust, have them carry out
the routine as usual. If, however, you have a non-family member putting
your child to bed, simply inform them in writing and review verbally
before you leave, exactly what the routine will be. I suggest skipping the
bath and just having the baby-sitter take a warm face cloth to wipe your
child's face after they have brushed their teeth. The rest of the routine
can be carried out as usual. Be sure to speak to your child about the
changes to the schedule before hand so they know what to expect.

If you are taking your child to a friend's house, simply take comforting items with you such as a blanket, pyjamas, or favourite stuffed animal.
Don't forget to bring along a couple of books to read. Again, in order
for this to be successful, you should inform your child before leaving
your house as to the change in routine that night. Tell them that when

you are ready to leave you'll simply carry them out to the car and tuck them into their own bed when you arrive home. Share a story here if you have one. I, for example, remember fondly when my parents used to do this with my sister and I. We used to love the feeling of being picked up and carried out to the car by our father when my parents stayed late at a friend's house. We would actually be awake but would pretend we were asleep because it was such a nice feeling. When dad finally laid us in our own beds the feeling of comfort and coziness was just awesome!

What is the appropriate hour to put your child to bed? According to most studies, on average, a pre-schooler should have a bed time of about 7 or 8 pm and school-aged children from 8 – 10 pm, obviously only increasing the hour if the child seems fine with it. Research suggests that children need to have between 10 – 12 hours of sleep a night. Sleep is not only the time when our body repairs and strengthens itself, but it is when our sub-conscious works through the days events. Therefore, a good night's sleep is important for both our physical *and* psychological well-being. If your school-aged child seems to be having trouble going to sleep at the assigned bedtime and wakes up easily the next morning, then you can change the bedtime to an hour later and see how they respond to waking up the next morning.

If you haven't had a routine in place or are struggling with putting your child to bed and keeping them there then start by having a family meeting. At the meeting tell your child that starting tonight things are going to work a little differently because sleep, other than food, is the number one thing a body needs to be happy. Explain the following system to them:

1) "I will warn you 5 minutes before I expect you to get your pyjamas on. After 5 minutes, I expect you to put on your pyjamas and head to the bathroom."

2) "I'll join you in the bathroom while you brush your teeth. If all goes well while you brush your teeth, I will have time to read you a story or tell you the story of your day. If you dawdle or whine I will not have time to (read you a story) and we'll have to try again the next night."

3) "Let's practise." Go through the routine. If they are uncooperative, remind them that this is exactly how things will work
   at bedtime therefore if they are uncooperative there will be no
   time for a story. They may say, "I don't care". Do not respond to
   this. Simply say, "Well, I would sure like to tell you a great story
   tonight. Let's see how things go."

That night, follow the routine. Go to your child and state that he
or she has 5 minutes before it's time to get his/her pyjamas on. After
5 minutes, go to him and say, "Time to get ready". Help him if need be
and do a diaper change if necessary. Please note that he may not be
particularly helpful or happy whilst you do this, but it shouldn't stop
you from getting the job done quickly. You may even consider leaving
him in his clothes rather than making this a huge issue at the beginning.
Following this step, take him to the bathroom, fix the toothbrush, and
while he brushes his teeth you can either compliment him on how
cooperative he is being or, if he is being uncooperative, state, "You are
(whining), so as we talked about at the family meeting, I won't have time
to tell you the story of your day." Even if he stops right away, do not
cave in. Tuck him in to his bed, say, "I love you. Have a good sleep. See
you in the morning", then close and secure the door, and leave him to
cry himself to sleep if need be. A quick way to secure the door is to
attach the plastic door handle covers you can buy at children stores.
You'll find that the next night will go more smoothly because of your
firmness tonight.

You may be wondering what the "Story of the Day" is. Basically you
start off like this:

"Once upon a time there was a child named _____ (your child's
name). He/she got out of bed in the morning and had _____ for breakfast. ..." Now you proceed to tell the "story" of your child's day. Keep it
simple and short (3-5 minutes) and include any outings, visits, surprises,
laughs or comments about things they learned. End the story like this:
"...and then he brushed his teeth cooperatively and there was time to
tell him the story of the day."

Summary

In order to have a happy, healthy child a child needs their sleep. In order to have their sleep, they need to have a well-established bedtime routine. A routine is doing the same things, in the same order, at the same time every day just before going to bed and to sleep. There may be nights when the routine might be upset a little due to baby-sitters or staying at a friend's house later, and this is good. Learning to work around a schedule at times allows the child to learn the art of flexibility. If you haven't had a routine or are struggling with your current routine, try the one given above, as many parents have had a lot of success with it. Just remember to stay consistent and don't be drawn in to their sweet requests for more time, one more hug, one more....consistency, as in all things is the key.

TELEVISION PRIVILEGES

Television has become very important in many family homes over the last 15 years. More and more, television is used as a babysitter or a way of escaping from life. Although I agree that there are some terrific programs on television for both adults and children, I strongly believe that we as a society are watching too much and are in the process, disconnecting from ourselves and our families.

Every mother knows that putting in a DVD or sitting a child in front of a television show is needed every once in a while, maybe even once a day. This is fine, however, the problem is that many children today are not able to sit and play by themselves for a half an hour. Their creativity and ability to think divergently has greatly diminished, and I blame TV and computer games for this. Do children re-enact TV programs when they play? Absolutely. But, do they create their own games and characters? Not so much. As a teacher I saw the repercussions of too much television during recess time. Over the past 14 years, I have seen the level of aggression on the playground increase greatly. No longer are kids creating galaxies or other worlds, they are wrestling and playing shooting games with guns and lasers. If they aren't involved in these activities, they are kicking around a soccer ball or walking around talking about how bored they are. This is always so sad for me to witness because I remember loving recess when I was a child. We would race outside and play in the jungle gym pretending we were in a space ship. Other exciting games were to use the natural ditches as our homes and pretend we lived in a big neighbourhood. Some of my fondest memories of school are during recess because of all the fun things we played. I still see some of this today, but do you know who these kids are? They are the ones whose parents have decided that video games are not as important as having free play time, reading or participating in individual or family activities.

As a culture I believe we have become scared to be in silence, or simply have music on while performing other tasks. It literally scares people when I suggest sitting down for ten minutes to practise breathing techniques. In order to become healthy human beings we need to learn to be with our thoughts, our souls, and hear the messages that we are being given on a daily basis.

One of the biggest gifts you can give your child is to teach them breathing techniques, journal writing, or meditating because it helps both their physical and psychological well-being. They will be better equipped to go out into the world and deal with the inevitable hardships that pass through everyone's lives at some point. I believe too, that the reason so many adults are on anti-depressants today is because they were not taught the techniques I mentioned above. All they know how to do is continue living the rat race, take prescription drugs or watch TV to get them by. I am not suggesting that everyone taking anti-depressants does not need them, however, I am suggesting that every single person could benefit from learning and practising some calming techniques. A great resource to look at is Dr. Andrew Weil's CD called, "Breathing: The Master Key to Self Healing". Listening to this CD will astound you. The physical benefits of breathing alone are quite shocking.

So, we want to teach our children how to be creative, imaginative, healthy individuals, right? How do we do this? I will speak about this more in the chapter on Family Traditions however the first step is to manage the amount of time your child spends in front of the television. Here are a few ideas to make this work.

1) Remember to be sure that no television privileges are given before all homework and teamwork tasks are completed. Television is their privilege only *after* these things are done.

2) Use television/DVD's as an occasional distraction for your toddler or pre-schooler. Once a day for a half hour or hour is fine, but more is unacceptable. Teach your child that playing by himself/herself is a very grown-up thing to do. I remember a time when I was four years old and I announced to my mom that I was bored. She was busy sewing something so she said, "Well, your sister always used to take toilet paper rolls and create things out of them. Sometimes she built houses, and sometimes she made people." She probably used this tactic because she knew I always wanted to be big like my sister, so off I went in search of toilet paper rolls and sat down for more than an hour creating people. My mom always showed how proud she was of me. This was so simple, yet so effective.

3) For older, school- aged children, give them a maximum of time to watch television throughout the week. My parents gave my sister and I a maximum of 6 hours a week. They then handed us a TV Guide and told us to choose the programs we would like to watch. We had to calculate how long our programs were and how best to distribute them throughout the week. Some nights were really great nights for TV, therefore we would watch a little more on those nights and less on others. We felt loved because they were thinking of our best interests and re-spected because they allowed *us* to create the schedule. When we were finished, they checked our lists and made sure none of our shows overlapped or were inappropriate. My sister and I were shocked at how great it felt to watch a show and then turn off the TV and find something else to do.

4) Some parents find that with their family's busy schedule there is no time for TV during the week. Others simply want their children to focus on school work during the week and therefore only allow TV on the weekends. If this suits your family values or dynamics, great! I would just caution one thing here. Just like you need down time after work, so does your child from schoolwork. Please be sure to find a perfect time for home-work to be done and then have it be finished. The rest of the night can be used for family bonding or individual play time.

Summary

Television and DVD's can be relaxing, entertaining and educational, however, the phrase "too much of anything is not healthy" applies here. We should not be looking to TV, DVD's, and computer games to be our sole form of relaxation, entertainment and education. Children learn to be imaginative, creative, and think more divergently when they are left alone to entertain or educate themselves. In addition to this, children need to learn, as we all do, that being alone in silence or with peaceful music on is necessary to have a healthy life. When all is calm and quiet we can hear our souls or a higher power speaking to us. Without the silence it is virtually impossible to hear the messages we are being given. Reading, journaling, meditating, or performing breathing techniques are some wonderful ways to achieve this. Why not put on some Mozart and bring out paints, crayons, and paper and just doodle? I strongly believe that if you change just one thing in your family, that this be it. You will be amazed at the difference not only in your children, but in yourself as well. So, turn off all those stimulating images and just "BE" for a while.

This concludes the Warding off Common Problems chapter. Can you see how dealing with issues before they arrive can really make a difference? If we are constantly in a state of "reactiveness" we can become exhausted and feel unempowered. We might start having doubts about our abilities as parents and begin to think badly of ourselves. This is not healthy and is, as you now know, unnecessary. Choose one issue every few months and make the necessary proactive changes. If you try to make too many changes to your family, everyone will feel overwhelmed. If, however, your family is running pretty smoothly already, but you want to tweak things in a few areas, by all means choose a couple of areas to change. Just be proactive, and think through how many changes your particular family can handle at this point and time.

PART 2

Family Time

Chapter Four

MAKING TIME FOR FAMILY

Families today are stressed to the limit. Many Moms and Dads are both working, kids are going to school, racing to their next game, practice or lesson, bills are coming in, cleaning needs to get done, meals need to be made, etcetera, etcetera. The list could go on and on. In our society, we are finding more stressed out and depressed people, as well as more crime, and less safety on our streets. This paints a pretty bleak picture, doesn't it? I know. At times, I find myself getting overwhelmed with all that seems wrong. Although, when I really stop and think about these issues, I smile, because I know with every inch of my being that one thing could have a real impact on changing or at least greatly improving many of the problems mentioned above. I strongly believe that if we as parents took charge and said, "ENOUGH IS ENOUGH!" and began allocating more time for family time and traditions, we, our children, and in turn our society would be much happier and safer.

Where do we even begin? You're probably thinking, "I'm just try- ing to discipline effectively, and now you're saying I have to do more?" Actually, my answer to that is no, you actually have to start doing less. Here's what I mean. Every May around Mother's Day, I ask my students to write in their journals. The topic is this: Give me advice on how to be a good mother. Think about whatever it is that your mother or guardian does for you that makes you feel happy and loved. The first time I did this, twelve years ago, I was shocked at how beautifully written these journal entries were. The classroom went silent immediately, and pencils wrote thoughtfully for longer than any other time they had written in their journals. The students cared about this topic wholeheartedly. They were happy as they remembered how they felt when their mothers made them feel loved. After this first time, I was no longer shocked, when every single year that followed, the classroom would fall silent and the writing would continue for that extended period of time. The best part of this assignment though, was when I would read their journals. I would sit at my desk after school sipping tea, and many times shedding a tear. There is a common theme among 99% of every single journal I have read over the past 12 years, and that is, that it is the **small things that have the biggest impact**. Kids appreciate and *remember* when you greet them at the door with arms outstretched for a hug. They also remember the notes you leave in their lunch bag and the special traditions you have created.

I have included this chapter because I feel that without it, I would be missing a piece of the family puzzle. Without slowing down, doing small things for your children and creating family traditions that you regularly share, you cannot have the quality of family life that you always dreamed about.

Did your family have any traditions that you particularly enjoyed and fondly remember? It could be as simple as your mother waking you up a certain way, or a gift she gave you every birthday. How about a dinner your family prepared whenever you had dinner guests? Think of one family tradition and notice how you feel inside. It's difficult to put into words, but it's comforting, isn't it? It made your family seem like such a unit. My family used to make a special meal for dinner guests. It was Curry chicken with rice, almonds, toasted sesame seeds, salad, and lemon pie for dessert. It was out of this world delicious, our guests always loved it, and we had fun preparing it together as a family. Every time I make it now, I feel so happy inside. I cannot explain why, I just do. Just as my students wrote, it is the most basic, simple things that children remember and love about their families, NOT all the lessons and activities to which they were driven.

I've had many a conversation with parents around the topic of feeling stressed from running around from activity to activity. They tell me they feel like they are always in need of a vacation. Many people step into the train of thought that more is better. "I want to give my child all the opportunities that I was offered, or not offered" is a phrase I hear all the time. Silken Laumann, Olympic gold medalist and author of "Child's Play: Rediscovering the Joy of Play in our Families and Communities" says, "While parents recognize the need for their kids to be active, their fears, along with their busy lives and the enormous societal pressure to make athletes, academics, and artists out of our children, have led us to schedule their every activity, driving them to and from soccer practise, piano lessons, and tutorials. Parents are trying so hard to give their children everything that they lose sight of the bigger picture. They keep them so busy with lessons when what they really need is time to just play."

I can tell you with all certainty that children are feeling stressed and overwhelmed too, because I have seen it and they have told me so. In weekly classroom meetings, many children have said, "I have no time to just play." I wish you all could have been in my classroom one year when every child was sharing their schedule with me. One boy blurted out, "I'm allowed to be a kid!" When I asked him to explain what he meant he said this: "When I get home, I directly take a shower, put on my pyjamas, do my homework, eat dinner, then have the rest of the night to play." You should have seen the intensity of his emotion. He was so thankful for his routine. All the students listened intently then began complaining once again about how they never get to do that. When I asked a few of the students if they had ever talked to their parents about how they felt they said, "My parents say, "You're just being lazy and a quitter". Yikes! Is this angst truly what we want for our children, folks? No, of course not! So why are we constantly running around with no down time? And why are the sources from which we and our children getting down time a television, computer, or video game? Let's slow down, unite our families, and all feel more full-filled and balanced. Limit your children's activities to one or two per week per season. A mother once asked me what one should do if their child truly *asked* to be involved in all the activities. My answer was simple, "You must be the parent then and teach them that that is not how to live a balanced life."

What follows in this chapter are some terrific ideas on how to achieve more balance in your family's life, how to deepen and strengthen your family, and how to create memories that will last forever in your children's minds.

DINNER TIME

Family dinners seem to have become a thing of the past. I say, Let's bring 'em back! Dinner time is a time when you can show as a family your appreciation for all your blessings, share disappointments, accomplishments and feelings and create memories that last forever. It is only tricky to make sure you eat together if you make it tricky. I refuse to accept it when people say, "It's impossible to eat together. Everyone has got something going on." Exactly. Family comes first and if everyone is running around then you cannot say that you and your partner make family a priority. It's as simple as that. It may come as a hard blow to those of you who are realizing right now, while reading this, that your family is not participating in family meals together, but once again, as Maya Angelou says, "You are doing the best that you know how, and when you know better you do better". Here's your opportunity to make a change.

Ideally, most of your dinners should be ones where everyone is present. Of course, the odd scheduling conflict might arise, but all in all work everyone's schedules around dinner time. I have many friends whose husbands are investment bankers. This job is a time consuming job and often requires them to stay at work a little later than the typical 5:00pm. Both of their husbands make it a rule to leave work by 6:30pm so that they are home for dinner at 7:00pm most nights. This sounds late I know, but both of my friends have made this a priority. If you have little ones, feed them, bathe them and then around the time dad gets home, give them a bottle to enjoy while the rest eat dinner. If you have older, school aged children, let them have a substantial snack after school, do their homework, have some downtime, then sit down to eat when dad gets home. Remember folks, this system of eating later is what is done in many countries. They all think we're strange for eating so early. In France, we ate dinner at 8:00pm or 8:30pm most nights! Whatever you and your husband come up with is your family's normal. Don't compare yourselves to the Smith family. Make eating together a priority **at least** 4 times per week.

Why is dinner time so important? It is one time, each day, when your family connects. Much can be accomplished at dinner time. Here are just a few ways to make meal time extra special and meaningful for your family.

1) Show your children and spouse that they are the most important people in your life – DO NOT ANSWER THE TELEPHONE DURING MEAL TIME! (Unless of course, you hear the caller leaving an emergency message) My husband taught me this. I used to jump up and sometimes be held on the phone for far too long. He would be sitting at the table, alone, finishing his meal, while I sat on the couch listening to someone else talk. One night he sat me down and said, "Look, family time is family time. This is an opportunity for us to be together. We need to make this a priority. Let's allow the answering machine to take a message during dinners, okay?" The fact that this meant that much to him really touched me. It made me feel loved and that he valued spending quality time with me. Ever since that night, it has been a rule in our house that no one answers the phone during dinner unless it's an emergency. Show your family how much you value them, and let that answering machine do its job.

2) Use dinner time as a time to get to know about your children's lives. It's important in this day in age that your children feel comfortable to talk you about their lives. Knowing who your children spend time with and how they spend that time is really critical in our world today. Many parents have complained to me about the one word answers they receive when they ask their child a question. They say, "I ask how his day was and he just says, 'Fine'. How do I get him to open up more?" As teachers, we have a variety of techniques we use when asking questions. Based on what type of response we want, we word the question differently. If you want specific answers then be sure to ask *specific* questions. For example, if you want to know who they are spending time with ask, "Who did you play with at recess today?" If you want to know what they are studying in Geography class, ask: "What did you learn in Geography class today?" If you want more back and forth discussion, then be sure to ask *open-ended* questions. Form a question where their

answer can not be a one word answer or a yes or a no. Phrases like, "Do you think….." or "Tell me about…" are perfect for this.

Deepak Chopra wrote a beautiful book called "The Seven Spiritual Laws for Parents". In this book he shows how to teach your children about core humanistic traits and how to understand the natural principles of life. Each day of the week has a trait attached to it. He shows how to model, teach and practise each trait in a natural, non-intrusive manner. It is an inspiring book that focuses on the true meaning of life and how to live more harmoniously in it. I highly recommend it to those of you looking to teach your children about compassion, generosity, intention, going with the flow, success, and personal purpose. Dinner time is a perfect opportunity to put his ideas into practise.

If this doesn't appeal to you, here are some questions I have created that I believe are very beneficial as well.

a) What did you do today that made you proud of yourself?
b) What kind of problem did you solve today?
c) Tell me about something you did alone today that you enjoyed.
d) Tell me about something you did with someone else today that you really enjoyed.
e) Tell me about something you found difficult to do? Easy to do?
f) Tell me about a mistake you realized you made? What did you do about it?
g) Tell me about a time today where you showed compassion towards yourself or someone else.
h) Tell me about a time today when you were generous. How did the other person look or react when you did this? How did you feel?

The key here is to make the questioning as natural as possible. Do not come across as if you are searching for something. Why not share an experience from your day and then ask about one they had. Let them know about a task you found really difficult and how you worked through that task. Then, ask them to share, or your husband. This way conversation flows, and you have just used dinner as a time to model how problems can be solved. You have shown them that it's not only they who feel frustrated at times. Another idea might be to assign a question to each day of the week. This way, each member will be consciously watching themselves so that they have something to share at the dinner table that night!

3) As mentioned in Chapter three, make dinner time a time to have fun and create lasting memories. Teach planning, organizing, entertaining and manners by having your family plan a dinner for another family. Or, simply plan a theme night just for your family. Find music, decorations, recipes, costumes, and movies that tie into that theme. For example, let's say your child is studying about Japan in school. Sit down as a family and find Japanese music off the internet. Discuss what could be bought or made to decorate the dining room. Search the internet or go to the library to collect Japanese recipes. Decide on any costumes you want to wear or have each person come up with their own and surprise each other on the night! I always like to have a movie to watch that goes with the theme. Depending on the age of your children, you could rent a foreign film, or a Japanese cartoon video. Or, how about renting a karaoke machine to sing the night away as is popular in Japan? The possibilities are endless and the themes can be too. When I lived in France, I had a Valentines theme night for the boys. We made Valentine shaped pizzas, made a special red juice, played Valentine BINGO and watched their favourite movie, "The Mask" for the hundredth time because I "loved" them. They were absolutely thrilled with the night. The next morning, the oldest, most reserved boy said, "Erin, thank you for a fantastic night. I'll never forget it." I'm not saying you have to do this every month (that would be stressful and might take away from the excitement), however, how about making it an every 3rd or 6th month event? Put it on your calendar at the beginning of the year. Just watch how excited your children will get when the date begins to get closer!

IDEAS FOR FAMILY INTERACTION

There are countless ways in which you can strengthen the bond you have with your family. Try some of the ideas below and see which ones work well for you. Make some of them your own family traditions, or simply set a time each night when you participate in some kind of family activity. You could even take turns deciding which activity to do. The point is to spend quality time together, with everyone relaxing and having fun. Doing this, you will be creating lasting memories and reducing the amount of time you and your family spend running around or watching endless hours of TV. Instead of feeling like a frazzled, disconnected family, you'll feel like a solid unit where the connection between you all grows each and every day.

1) Every family member grabs a book/novel and reads in the same room for a half hour. At my house we love to have Mozart playing in the background.
2) Sit together in a circle and do a 10 minute breathing exercise. Try using Dr. Andrew Weil's CD called, "Breathing: The Master Key to Self Healing" as a guide, or any other CD or cassette you and your family enjoy.
3) Play board games or cards together.
4) Watch a movie together on a school night.
5) Go out to dinner. Take turns choosing where to eat.
6) Go see a play, music or comedy event together.
7) Go to the library. Be sure your children understand that this is time for you personally as well. You have the right to peruse books that you are interested in – you are NOT obligated to hang out in the children's area. If you are the only adult or you have an only child, take turns looking at books. Let your child pick some first so he/she can read them while you do your looking.
8) Go on a picnic – even on a school night! How about picnicking in the backyard?
9) Go on short weekend trips to just get away, change the routine, and relax on a deeper level. Leave those weekend errands until next weekend!

10) Fly kites in the park.
11) Throw or kick a ball around in the park.
12) Go for after-dinner walks.
13) Build a snowman together.
14) Go swimming at the local pool.
15) Have "Friday Cocktail Hour". The family I lived with in France did this. We all looked forward to Friday because of it. In the winter, we lit the fireplace, dimmed the lights, and lit a few candles in the family room. Then we poured juice in cheap wine glasses for the kids and wine for us in more fancy ones. A cheese platter and baguette were then placed on the coffee table for all to enjoy. In the summer, lemonade would be given to the boys to enjoy while they played in the yard as we adults sat with our glass of wine on the patio to chat. I just loved this, and I know the boys did too.
16) Volunteer together. Children can, by nature, be very self-centered. Our job as parents is to show them the world outside their own needs and wants. Search the internet or phone book for your city's volunteer centre. Often they list specific volunteer ideas that are well suited to families. As well, ask your children to brainstorm ways they could volunteer their time and energy. Ex. Shovel someone's sidewalk, cut a neighbour's lawn, offer to baby-sit for free. Another great tradition can be to sort through their toys at each birthday and give away any outgrown ones to Goodwill or charity. These opportunities will not only help build your child's self-esteem, compassion and empathy, but will help ensure that our communities are filled with responsible, caring citizens. I thank you all in advance.
17) Build a puzzle together
18) Sing songs or play music together
19) Draw, paint or create a piece of "art" together. This can be as simple as a large painting which can be hung in the home or as elaborate as a mosaic table top.
20) Bake something together.

ONE ON ONE TIME

As mentioned earlier, my students have told me that it is the small things that make the biggest impact on them. A common piece of advice given to me in many journals was this: "Be sure to spend one on one time with each child. Some of my most favourite times are when my mom takes me to the park and we just walk and talk without my sister or brother."

Again, this does not have to be every week, but it should be scheduled in so that it happens at least every month or month and a half. Your one on one time, so my students say, can be as simple as sitting together in bed and watching a movie or TV show, going for a walk, or playing your child's favourite game. The point is, children need and love to have their mother or father's undivided attention. The bonds that can be created here are immeasurable. Spending quality time together will help you keep in touch with the emotional stages of their lives, which is invaluable when the teenage years arrive! You will want and need them to feel totally at ease to talk to you about their daily joys and struggles. The bonus to this as well is that your children will be happier and in turn be more willing to abide by the rules of your family.

Be sure to keep this date. If, for some very important reason, you must cancel this date, be sure to sit your child down and explain the reason why. As well, look at the calendar and reschedule in the not too distant future. By doing this, you will show your child that they at times need to be flexible and understanding but that you care about them and look forward to the time you spend together.

FAMILY CALENDARS

Family calendars are super ways to keep your family on track and organized. Using one ensures that you are successfully making time for special traditions, one on one time, and time simply for yourself and partner. Here is how they work.

- Make the first Sunday of each month or if it works better, the last Sunday of each month, your family calendar meeting time. Bring out any school calendars, notices, or sport schedules, and plot, or have your children plot, depending on their age, all the activities occurring that month.
- Be sure to schedule in monthly date nights with your husband or wife. (more about this in Chapter 5) Children need to see that your relationship is a priority and that dates are a way mom and dad keep their marriage healthy. What a great model for them to use in their future relationships!
- Add in any family theme nights, weekend getaways, or exercise commitments you or your husband have for yourselves. Your exercise commitment can be as simple as going down to the basement for a workout, however, just be sure it goes on the calendar because it will model a healthy lifestyle and that time alone is important too.
- Put your personal appointments on the calendar as well. For example, a spa day or coffee date with your sister, brother, or friend, and of course, the one-on-one date with each of your children.
- VERY IMPORTANT: if you notice that your calendar is jam packed and you feel your pulse begin to race already, then see what you can cancel. DO NOT cancel quality time with your children, husband or self. These are necessities, not luxuries. Commitments to go to school events, bake for school or charity functions or dinner invitations you receive can be cancelled or rescheduled for a later date. As well, if your family has planned a theme night near the beginning of the meeting but you notice there are simply too many obligations in the month, discuss when a better time might be. Your children will feel extremely empowered by the fact that you care about their opinions.

ALONE TIME IS IMPORTANT TOO

Although what I'm about to say might seem contradictory to everything I have written about in this chapter so far, hang on and hear me out.

I'll begin with a quote from Hooding Carter. He said, *"There are two lasting bequests we can hope to give our children. One of these is roots; the other, wings."* Parents are the ones who give roots via family experiences, traditions and special customs. We are also the ones who have the responsibility to teach our children how to be self-sufficient, capable, and how to have a healthy self-esteem. I have already spent most of this chapter discussing how to give children roots; I now want to spend a little time showing you how simple it is to give your children "wings". What follows is a list of ways you can accomplish this.

1) Don't go to every single sporting practise. I know, I know, I hear the gasps already. Take a deep breath and read on. In my opinion, dropping your child off every once in a while teaches them that they are capable even without you. As well, I believe this experience makes the times when you *are* there even more special. If you try to do everything, what you are subtly teaching your child is that only *they* matter and no one else. Could you not give them a hug and kiss, say, "Have fun", and tell them that you are going to run some errands, or have your own special time while they play? Get rid of that guilt, folks. I'm giving you permission. As long as you ask them about the practise when you pick them up and listen intently and joyfully, they will be happy. You have shown confidence in them, you have shown them how to be independent, and that they are capable individuals. You have also modelled how to live a balanced life. Of course go to their games, cheer them on, give hugs and high fives, just don't model that you are not important and only they matter. We don't need any more self-indulged people in this world. The bonus here is that you are managing your time effectively and are able to fit in things that otherwise you would not have time for. How about going to the gym while they are at practise? How about getting a manicure or reading a book at a coffee shop? How about using the time to write a personal,

hand written note to a family member or friend? How about a beer with your buddies? It's a win – win situation. Try it. I promise, you will thank me for this advice.

2) Create an "Alone Time" hour. This is a super idea for mothers who stay home during the day with their young children. Schedule in an hour, the same hour, everyday, that is called "Alone Time". At first your child might get bored or insist you play with them but eventually they will find ways to entertain themselves. Suggest ideas to them. For example, they could paint, build things with "Lego", mould "Play Dough", make a craft, draw, paint, take pictures of nature with a disposable camera, read, kick a ball around, play in the sand box or simply play with their action figures and dolls.

It is vitally important for your child's personal and academic success to learn at an early age that quiet, alone time is healthy and beneficial.

As best-selling author Elaine St. James states in her book "Simplify Your Life with Kids", "Alone time helps children get in touch with their feelings, review the past, contemplate the present and make plans for the future." She goes on to say, "Teach your children to appreciate solitude. As you limit their use of TV, video games, and the phone, they'll stop needing the stimulation of electronic media and learn to rely on their own inner resources." Deepak Chopra sees the need for silence as essential because it allows us to connect with our spirit. He says, "Children need to learn that silence is the home of the spirit. All other voices speak out loud, but spirit communicates without making a sound. Only when we are silent can we hear its wisdom."

From a teacher's perspective, I want to speak to the academic success that "Alone Time" can bring. When children are left to create and think on their own, they develop the part of the brain where divergent thinking takes place. If allowed to be alone and entertain themselves or to solve problems themselves such as how to get their sandcastle to stay upright, they will gain the necessary thinking skills needed in so many subject areas. In Language Arts and Science students are expected to infer, in Math they are expected to solve word problems, and in

Geography/History they are expected to form opinions. All the skills needed to be successful in these subjects are built upon from an early age. If we provide the opportunities for this to happen while they are young, we give them a greater amount of time for learning and divergent thinking to develop.

Summary

Hopefully after reading this chapter you see the need for creating at least one family tradition and are really excited to put it into action right away. In addition, I hope you understand the importance of taking the pressure off you and your children in order to create a more peaceful, balanced life. Alone time is not just a good idea, it is essential. Remember that using a family calendar is the best way to make sure all the good things, like spending one on one time with your child or exercising are going to occur each month. Discard all the unnecessary activities, and release your guilt about having to do it all. Nothing is more important in this lifetime than leading a healthy and happy existence and teaching your children how to do it too.

PART 3

You

Chapter Five

ALL ABOUT YOU

You've all heard it before, "If you don't take care of yourself, then you won't be good for anyone else". It is time for you to finally "get this". My goal in this chapter is to put into place the last piece of the family puzzle. I want you to feel as capable in this piece as you are with the discipline piece.

You WERE a person with interests, talents and dreams before you got married and had children, and you still ARE a person with interests, talents and dreams. They might have been neglected lately, but they're still there needing and desiring attention. This chapter's focus is on rediscovering you and how that relates to the happiness and success of your family life.

Each of us has many roles that we play. We are a partner, a sister, a brother, a son, a daughter, a father, a mother, an employee and a friend.

However, I want you to look at yourself a little deeper than these roles. Who are you REALLY? If I asked you to list 10 words that would describe who you are, what would they be? Try it.

1.   6.
2.   7.
3.   8.
4.   9.
5.   10.

Look over your list. Did you list hobbies, talents, personality traits and interests of yours? If you did, and your list seems to truly represent who you are, then continue to the next activity. If you feel you can be more specific then redo this activity. Your list cannot be exactly the same as above. Some words might be the same, but change at least 3 so you get really specific about who you are.

1.   6.
2.   7.
3.   8.
4.   9.
5.   10.

Here's the next activity I want you to do. Look at the words in each section of the "Life Circle" to the right. Read each word out loud. As you read each word, stop and think about what that word represents to you.

LIFE CIRCLE

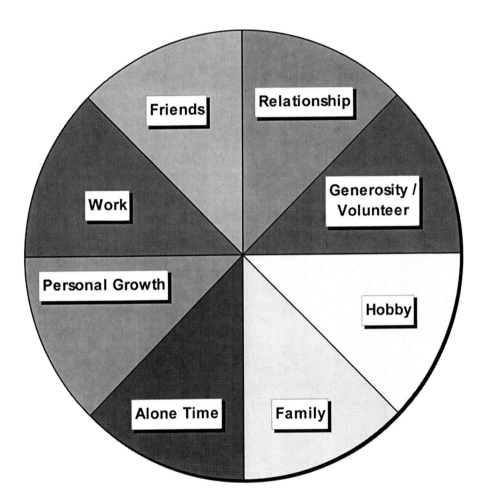

Now, here comes your reality check. Read each word again and give a specific example from a day this month where you gave intentional energy to what each word represents. For example: If I read the word, "Hobby" I would give an example of when I sat down at the piano to play some of my favourite songs. If I then read "Family" I would give an example of when my family went for a bike ride and picnic in the country-side. For "Generosity" I would give the example of the free babysitting

I offered a friend. "Alone Time" would be when I went to a coffee shop to read my book and "Personal Growth" when I listened to an audio by my favourite personal growth author. "Work" would be taken care of easily since I run www.erinparenting.com daily as well as write articles for my *Juggling Family* Life Newsletter and Blog, and finally, if I read the word "Relationship" I would give the example of going to a jazz club with my husband. Do you get the picture? Now, try it yourself.

Contribution/Volunteer _____

_____

Hobby _____

_____

Family _____

_____

Alone Time _____

_____

Personal Growth _____

_____

Work _____

_____

Friends _____

_____

Relationship _____

_____

Were you able to give an example for every word? Did you have many examples for one word, but few if any for others? Reflect on this activity below.

_____
_____
_____
_____
_____
_____
_____
_____
_____
_____
_____
_____
_____
_____
_____
_____
_____
_____
_____
_____
_____
_____
_____
_____
_____
_____
_____
_____
_____
_____
_____
_____
_____
_____

Mothers and fathers, particularly mothers, tend to put their kids, work, and other people's needs first, and leave themselves and their needs and wants second. This is unhealthy and wrong. You were born for a reason. It wasn't just so that you could be someone's mother, partner, friend, etcetera. You were born to live out your destiny. YOU matter, YOU count. You are entitled to live fully, not to feel overwhelmed and stretched too thin. We allow ourselves to fall into ruts and sometimes even convince ourselves that this is just the sacrifice you must make when you decide to have a family. I'm here to tell you that this is NOT what life is meant to be like with a family, and that you have the power to enjoy a blissful life while having a family. Yes, there are more things to do and get organized when you have children, but if you work things right, a blissful life is absolutely achievable.

One of the major stressors in a family is children having a lack of discipline and the chaos that that can bring. Therefore, I chose to put the chapter on achieving discipline at the beginning of this book. With discipline in place, much more is achievable. The topic of creating family traditions came second because traditions deepen and strengthen the bonds you will have created with your family. Your family life will seem simpler, and a sense of what is truly important will have taken hold of you. As well, in that chapter, I teach how to use a calendar to schedule in time for your family. Learning this makes you ready for this last chapter, which is to realize the final action necessary to feeling happy and fully successful in your family life. The last piece of the puzzle is to understand that YOU are important and that your desires ARE valid. Putting this realization into practise will fill you up so that you are whole enough and have energy enough to give your family the best of who you are and what you have to offer.

The first step to adding this last piece of the puzzle is to go back to that calendar you and your family began using, and place on there activities that would fulfill each of the words on the "Life Circle". Does this mean you have to schedule in five activities per word? Absolutely not! Just be sure that on your calendar you have at least one activity to represent each word. There are on average 30 days in a month. If you have one activity listed for each word, that's only 8 days. You are left with 22 days to do whatever your soul desires or whatever obligations you must fulfill. You see, many of us just feel stressed because we keep thinking about all the things we should do. If you take that one day at the beginning of the month to plan your calendar you will be totally amazed at how much stress will be lifted off your shoulders. Your mind won't be cluttered and life will run more smoothly and feel more en-riched than it ever has. No longer will you commit to something only to find out you already said you would do something for someone else that day, and end up feeling stressed and resentful. You will now say, "Let me check my calendar and get back to you." How simple! I promise you this works. I have been where many of you are, and have walked to the other side.

Go to an office supplies store today or tomorrow and buy yourself a monthly calendar if you haven't already. Fill it out with your family and put it up in your kitchen or main area of action. Already using a calendar? Then go to it NOW and add on your activities to match each word on the "Life Circle".

By using a monthly calendar we have made sure that you will be on time for appointments, have special time with your partner and family and enough alone time for your own needs. The most important thing to realize is this – life with children does change your life. You must understand that you will not be able to flop down on that couch when-ever you want, but.... by scheduling in the "Life Circle" categories, you can reassure yourself that you really do have time for everything that is truly important in life, even if each item is not as much as you would like right now. The keyword here is *balance,* and by using this calendar you will be achieving just that – balance.

I want to share with you another tip that I use to keep me on track on a daily basis. This idea came from my teaching experience. You see, as a teacher, the list of things to do is endless. One year I became so stressed that I broke out in hives and my lips began to swell to triple their size. I'm serious! Crying every night to my husband as well as feeling completely overwhelmed and depressed became my reality. If I was going to survive I knew I needed to gain some control over what I could, both in my work and personal life.

Every year I buy a day timer. In there I write down things I want to accomplish each day. These things can be as simple as meditating, exercising, reading my novel for 20 minutes, filling out insurance forms, taking mail to the post office, or phoning a friend who I haven't spoken to in a while; the point is that I get the clutter out of my head and out onto paper. Usually I cross off each item when it's completed, however, I allow for flexibility; sometimes things come up which don't allow me to complete everything. My plan each day is to do the things I absolutely must or absolutely want to achieve then anything that may not be urgent is moved to the next day's list. Try not to let any item get pushed off more than a week. If you're ignoring doing something, it is causing you unconscious stress and that is not your goal. Just do it and cross it off your list, your body will thank you for it.

Summary

By putting these simple steps into practise you will feel happier and less stressed in no time. Take as long as you need to complete the exercises I provide and reflect on the "Life Circle" until you have a clear picture of what each section means to you. Once you really know what is important for you in your life, get out that calendar and start assigning an activity for each section. Distribute them evenly throughout the month, then sit back and watch how nicely that month unfolds. You will wish you learned about this technique sooner. Enjoy!

FINAL SUMMARY

The puzzle is now complete, folks. You have probably experienced a shift in your thoughts while reading and processing this book. I am positive you are feeling better about yourself as a mother, partner, and human being because of these shifts as well as from the implementation of the strategies taught. There will be days when you snap at your child instead of using the "Tricks of the Trade", and there might even be times when you realize you haven't been making enough time for yourself or your family. However, *most* of the time you *will* be achieving balance and that is what is important - you have the knowledge now to fall back on.

Give yourself and your partner a big hug for making all the positive, important changes you have made. It has taken courage, effort and a true desire to live more fully and be a great parent that has gotten you to where you hopefully are now, or are soon headed. Congratulations, and from the bottom of my heart, I wish each and every one of you the family life you have always wanted.

Enthusiastically yours,

Erin

Erin A. Kurt

Appendix

MY RESPONSES TO THE SCENARIOS

Scenario One

This is obviously a situation where the Nintendo Game (object) is the cause. So, the first thing I would do is go into the room and **describe,** in my **normal voice,** what the boys need to do. First, I would turn off the TV and have the boys look at me so I have their full attention. I would then say, "Brian and Jeremy, you need to figure out a way you both can be happy. No more name calling or physical contact." Now, I pose my **choices** question. You can work out a compromise or you can spend 10 minutes in time out thinking about how you can compromise. What is your choice?" I would turn the TV on and walk away.

Of course, in these scenarios, I told you they would continue the behaviour. So, in this case, they begin fighting again. I would walk back in, take the object away, and tell Jeremy to go to the Dining room and Brian to the Living Room. **(consequence)** "I want to talk to you in the kitchen after time is up." I have enough time to do a follow-up talk right away so I call them to the kitchen after 10 minutes.

The boys come in and I say, "Arguing and hitting did not turn out to be a good choice. How can we make this work? What could you do differently next time you need to decide which game to play?" Jeremy replies, "It's impossible with him. He always wants to get his own way." I make sure I don't allow him to engage me in a debate so I ask him the question again, "I repeat, what could you do differently next time to decide? You are both intelligent and I know you can come up with a reasonable way to solve this problem." Brian says, "We could put the names of the games in a hat and pick one."

"That's a good idea," I say. "Jeremy, do you have anything to add to that or maybe you have a different idea?"

"I say we write our choices on different coloured paper like orange and blue and if two blues get picked in a row, we pick again until we get an orange."

"Does that sound fair to you Brian?" I ask.

"Yeah," he responds.

"These are great solutions. Can you handle playing together now?" Both boys reply with a yes and off they go to find coloured paper.

This is the ideal situation because I had time. However, if I didn't have time to do this discussion, I would have told them to play separately, (none on the Nintendo of course) and do my talk at bedtime. Here, they are left understanding that fighting isn't acceptable and that they are capable of finding positive solutions to their problems.

Scenario Two

Right after Kristy announces where she is going I say, "Alright, 6 o'clock is fine. See you at 6:00." The only reason I accepted Kristy *telling* me instead of *asking* me is that she is a teenager now and I am trying to give her more freedom in terms of making her own choices. She has proved to me that she can handle more freedom therefore I trust her to be back on time. If Kristy was younger I would insist that I be asked.

When Kristy arrives late I **describe** the behaviour I expect. "Kristy, you told me that you would be home at 6 o'clock. If you want the right to tell me when you will be back then you have the responsibility of keeping your word.

Of course, in this scenario, she's late again. I would say, "Kristy, I'm really disappointed. I spoke to you before about this being a privilege. Do you want to be able to make decisions on your own, or have me make them for you? She responds, "Make my own." I say, "Then let this be the last time you are late. You're smart, figure out a way to make this work."

For this example she arrives late again, but has many excuses. All I say is, "We've talked about this. Being late again shows me you can't handle this privilege of freedom. You will be staying home doing a quiet activity after school for the next two weeks. We'll try again after that. (**consequence**)

Kristy is upset. She tries to show me I'm not being fair by saying, "I didn't mean to be late. Honest! We were just having a really important talk and I lost track of time. Having me stay at home is stupid. I'm not a baby." My only reply is one of encouragement. "I know you're not and that's why next time you'll make sure you are home when you say you will be." I then change the topic by asking my husband a question so Kristy has some time to mull all this over in her mind. I treat her no differently because of her being late. It's over now. No grudges.

Scenario Three

Daniel is trying to play a control game here by only turning the stereo down a little. I have already **described** the behaviour I want in a **normal voice** so now I state my **choices** question. "Daniel, how high does the volume go on your stereo?"

"I don't know, 80. Why?"

"You can either turn down the volume to 20 or you can turn it off altogether and I keep it with me for a week. What would you like to do?" Angrily, Daniel turned it down but only to 25. My only response is to unplug the stereo, take it in my arms, and say, "You'll get this back in a week." (**consequence**)

It is extremely tempting to react to Daniel's defiant behaviour but I just keep telling myself that that is what he really wants, to upset me. If I can control myself and just focus on the 4 steps, he will learn that I do what I say, and this breeds respect. As well, I would not treat him differently because of this. I definitely wouldn't be taking him out for ice-cream or going out of my way to be especially nice to him, but I also wouldn't give him the silent treatment or name call. He would learn how to treat people just by watching how I treated him. Later that night, or possibly the next day, I would take time to sit with Daniel and speak to him about how we treat people in our household. I would expect an apology. This conversation is more appropriate at this time since both tempers have lowered, and you have had an opportunity to model what respect looks and sounds like. When you come to someone expressing your hurt while you're angry, they will simply try and defend themselves, however, if you model how you want to be treated and then discuss this with someone in a calm manner, they will most probably feel regretful for their behaviour, and an apology will be more heartfelt. This technique works especially well with teens.

Scenario Four

It is easy to figure out what is causing the problem; it's an object, the backpack. However, more than that, it's a lack of responsibility. In cases like this I would first **describe** the behaviour that he needed in a **normal voice**. "Christopher, you have been forgetting your backpack a lot lately. It looks like you need to come up with a solution to that problem. We'll talk about solutions tonight. As for now, it looks like you are going to have to face the consequence of getting 10% off." This is not what he wanted to hear. He responded by crying and saying, "Mom, you gotta bring me this paper. I worked so hard on it and I just can't get 10% off. Please, I won't ask you to do this ever again, I promise." My heart is aching to help him but I have to tell myself that I will not be teaching him anything if I bring him the paper. I decide to give my **choices** question but in a very heartfelt way. "Christopher, I hear you. This is not a nice experience, I know. I am very sure you won't do this again. You have a choice here. You can accept the 10% off (**consequence**) and bring your assignment in first thing tomorrow, or you can try discussing options with your teacher. What are you going to do?" He responded with, "I don't want any of those choices. I want you to bring me my backpack just this once!" Now he is trying to engage me so I cut him off. "That is not one of your choices, and I don't appreciate your tone. I know you'll make the right choice out of the options you do have. I love you. Now go discuss this with your teacher, she'll appreciate that." Still not happy, Christopher says, "Thanks a lot!" and hangs up the phone. I know in my heart he knows I love him and that I have made the right decision even though it was extremely difficult to see him have to learn this tough life lesson. Later, probably after school, I would ask Christopher about which decision he made and how the teacher reacted. I would praise him for having the maturity to speak to his teacher personally instead of just leaving it, and letting the teacher discover his missing assignment on her own. In addition to this, I would discuss his tone while he spoke to me. I would remind him that it goes totally against our household beliefs about how we treat one another. I would expect an apology.

Scenario Five

The cause of this situation is dirty objects, but in reality, if she is wants to go to her friend's house without cleaning up, the cause now turns out to be an abuse of a privilege. I would first **describe** in a **normal voice**, the behaviour I wanted. "Caroline, before you begin getting ready for your sleepover, you need to clean your room. That means all your clothes folded neatly in your drawers or hung up in the closet, all dirty dishes washed and put away, all dressers, night tables, and desks dusted and the floor vacuumed. Do you need me to write that down for you so you remember everything?" Caroline says no, so I walk away. Later, I notice she is in the bathroom getting ready so I go check her room. It is tidier, but it doesn't look like she vacuumed and her clothes are just stuffed in her drawers. I return to the bathroom and state her **choices** question. "Caroline, I looked at your room and there are some things that are not done the way I asked. Let's go to your room and go through the list." We go through the list and I point out what was done properly. Then, I say, "You need to finish the job correctly or stay home tonight doing it. What is your choice?" Angrily, she exclaims, "Mom, I can do this tomorrow. It's no big deal. I just have to vacuum and fold a few clothes. I'll do it tomorrow."

"That is not a choice. I offered you two. Which one do you choose?"

"Fine! I'll clean it now." (**consequence**)

"Thanks," I say, and walk out. When Caroline is leaving I am sure to give her a hug and say, "You did a great job, sweetie. Have fun at your sleepover."

Acknowledgements

To my amazing husband Ilker. Meeting you was an absolute dream come true. Every day I spend with you brings me so much joy. Your constant love and support allows me to live this life to the fullest. I love you so incredibly much.

To my son Emre Michael. You are such an incredible dream come true. I waited a long time for you, but now I have a deeper understanding as to why it took so long for you to arrive; it was so that I could have the time to write this book. Watching you and spending time with you inspires me each and every day. I love you and am so proud of who you are.

To my mom and dad. What can I say? You two have been my cheerleaders from day one. You told me and continue to tell me that I can do anything and that I have a gift to share. I will never forget my incredible childhood. The way you raised me, the traditions we shared…they are in this book. I love you both so much. Thank you for your support during this whole process.

To my sister Jana. What a special relationship we share. The memories of our childhood will stay with me forever. All the games we played, all the adventures we had, all the pains we shared – I love you so deeply, sissy. Having you as a sister is one of the biggest gifts I have been given in this lifetime.

No one accomplishes anything great by themselves – they always have some help or support. I am blessed to have had help and support from some amazing people in my life. My deepest thanks goes out to the following friends and family who helped me with a major part of this book. You know who you are, but I promised! Anne, Asha, Allison, Beatriz, Barbara, Blaire, Bryn, Christy, Cecilia, Charmaine, Debra, Dirk, David, Don, Elizabeth, Ellen, Fumika, Gillian, Helen, Janet, Jennifer, Jeff, Kate, Kelly, Laurie, Laara, Michelle D., Michelle K., Nicky, Patricia, Robin, Serena, Sea, Sacha, Sarah, Shauna, Tina, Tanya, Tammy, Tracey R., Tameeza and of course…Ilker. How wonderful it is to have you in my life – thank you.

To Izabela. Thank you for taking the lovely photos of me and for all your support and friendship over the past year.

Dedication

To all the children and parents I have worked with over the years. I consider it a blessing and an honour to have had the opportunity to work with you. It is because of you that I was able to write this book, and for that I will be eternally grateful.

Author Biography

Erin A. Kurt, B.Ed, received a degree in education at the University of Alberta in Edmonton, Canada. She has been a teacher in four different countries and a nanny in yet another. A freelance writer, she is also the president of Erin Parenting, an online business where she provides simple, easy-to-implement techniques that help parents create the family life they truly want. She is also the president of Celia and Cedric, Inc., where she is developing the educational products line, "Read and Bake." She holds regular teleseminars where people from all over the world call in to take part in her workshops and offers a free weekly newsletter to people who have subscribed on her website, www.erinparenting. com. Recently, she was featured in *Families* magazine in the UK. She lives with her family in Windsor, Berkshire, United Kingdom.

For further support and help visit: www.erinparenting.com

To read Erin's "*Juggling Family Life*" Blog visit: http://erinparenting.com/jugglingfamilylifeparentingblog/

LaVergne, TN USA
29 June 2010
187799LV00008B/125/P